Mich Turner
of LITTLE VENICE CAKE COMPANY

party cakes

PHOTOGRAPHY BY JANINE HOSEGOOD

UNIVERSE

I dedicate this book to my boys—
Phil, Marlow and George.
With Love Forever.

First published in the United States of America in 2007 by
Universe Publishing
A Division of Rizzoli International Publications, Inc.
300 Park Avenue South
New York, NY 10010
www.rizzoliusa.com

Originally published in the United Kingdom as
Fantastic Party Cakes in 2007 by
Jacqui Small LLP,
An imprint of Aurum Books Ltd
7 Greenland Street
London NW1 0ND

Publisher Jacqui Small
Editorial Managers Kate John and Judith Hannam
Editor Madeline Weston
Designers Maggie Town and Beverly Price
Photographer Janine Hosegood
Production Peter Colley

2007 2008 2009 2010 / 10 9 8 7 6 5 4 3 2 1

ISBN: 978-0-7893-1562-5

Library of Congress Control Number: 2007924706

Printed in China

contents

introduction Welcome to my second book showcasing a collection of *Party Cakes*. A fantastic party requires a fantastic cake and this book will provide ideas for every occasion. In the chapter *Delicious Treats*, I have included a range of gorgeous base-cake recipes which can be enjoyed in their own right for a special weekend afternoon tea. Alternatively, they can be used in the first two chapters for bite-size iced and chocolate-covered cakes for summer banquets, Christmas canapé parties, and baby showers, or small party cakes for more formal occasions including weddings, anniversaries, birthdays, and Christmas. You also will find a mouthwatering selection of fluffy desserts to choose from for lunch and dinner parties including cheesecakes, roulades, and meringues. I finish with a collection of beautifully hand-decorated pastries and cookies that make fabulous gifts or table centerpieces.

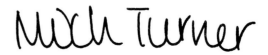

decorated delights

decorated delights There is something rather endearing about these individually covered or decorated cakes and bites. These beautiful designs are very special as they have "just for me" appeal. Befitting any celebration, they are sure to be a talking point or a lasting reminder of a fantastic party. I have created these designs using the recipes featured in the chapter *Delicious Treats*. Bake the cakes in a square pan for ease of stamping out rounds or cutting out squares. A single layer 8-inch square cake will yield sixteen individual 2-inch round or square cakes or twenty-five 1½-inch canapé-sized cakes.

chocolate boxes

These gorgeous little chocolate boxes are a very sophisticated way of serving a delicious chocolate-almond torte, sandwiched with espresso buttercream. They work equally well in white or milk chocolate. Cut into a perfect cube then surround it with tempered chocolate panels, and finish with an organza ribbon and a pretty label.

you will need

2-inch cube cakes covered in chocolate or espresso buttercream

dark chocolate—allow 5 oz. per cake

sharp knife

organza ribbon $5/8$-inch wide—allow 20 inches per cake

pretty cards

method

1 Temper the dark chocolate as shown in the techniques on page 147. Spread the chocolate out onto a marble slab or stainless steel tray to a depth of about $1/8$ inch. Once the chocolate has just set, use the templates on page 153 to cut out 2 short sides, 2 long sides, and 1 lid for each cake.

2 Fix the 2 short sides first onto opposite sides of one cake—they should adhere to the buttercream. Then fix the 2 longer sides on the two remaining sides before applying the lid.

3 Starting with the center of the ribbon in the center of the lid, wrap up the cake and tie the ribbon, fixing the pretty card into place. Finish all the cakes in the same way.

4 Serve on square plates. These cakes will keep for a few days once completed as they are shelf stable.

tip

These cakes are quite difficult to handle—try this size first before attempting to make them any smaller. A collection of 3 cubes in white, milk, and dark chocolate can make a stunning gift presented in a box.

marbled chocolate truffles

I first served these decadent and scrumptious marbled-chocolate truffles at the launch of my first book, *Spectacular Cakes*. They proved such a success with the guests that I knew they should feature in the second book. Use a combination of cake flavors such as banana butterscotch (page 85), chocolate and almond (page 90), or chocca mocca pecan (page 95) with marbled chocolates for a special canapé party.

you will need

1½-inch round cakes

chocolate scrolls and fans decoration

white chocolate plastique (first coat)—allow 1½ oz. per cake

white, milk or dark chocolate (top coat)—allow 2 oz. per cake

fork

method

1 Make the chocolate decorations following the technique on page 147. Cover the 1½-inch round cakes with an initial coat of white chocolate plastique as shown in the techniques on page 149 .

2 In 3 separate bowls, temper white, milk, and dark chocolate. Set the cakes on a wire rack with a sheet of nonstick parchment paper underneath. Using a large metal spoon or small ladle, spoon tempered chocolate over the cakes until fully covered as shown. Gently tap the rack to settle the chocolate.

3 Before the chocolate sets, dip a fork in a contrasting chocolate and marble over the cake creating interesting swirls as shown. Once the chocolate begins to set, decorate the top of each truffle with a chocolate decoration. Allow the cakes to set before using a metal spatula to transfer the cakes to a serving plate.

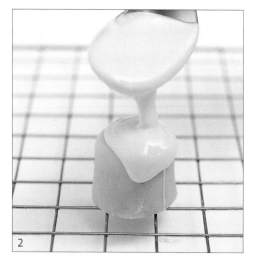

white chocolate pearls

These white chocolate-covered decorated cakes are charmingly chic for a wedding buffet. They look good presented on a large cake stand and served, one per guest, for dessert. They also make perfect take-home wedding favors presented in clear plastic boxes.

you will need

2-inch square cakes

white chocolate plastique—allow 6 oz. per cake for 2 coats and a fan

confectioners' sugar, for dusting

small rolling pin

pastry bag

tempered white chocolate for the pearls

cream grosgrain ribbon ⅝-inch wide—allow 8 inches per cake

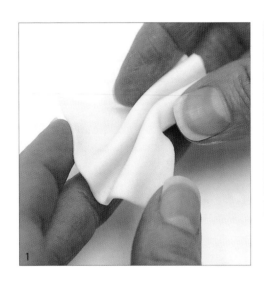

method

1 Lightly knead the white chocolate plastique on a work surface dusted with confectioners' sugar. Roll out a 2½-inch square very thinly and gently mold it into a fan shape as shown; pinch the base and trim it with a sharp knife. Make one for each cake (note, the picture on the right shows two fans on the cake).

2 Cover each 2-inch square cake with an initial covering of white chocolate plastique followed by a top coat as shown in the techniques on page 149.

3 Fill a pastry bag with a small amount of cooled tempered white chocolate. Snip the end of the pastry bag. Fix a length of cream grosgrain ribbon around the base of each cake and pipe random "pearls" over the top and sides. Fix the fans into position on the top of each cake.

fondant diamonds

Fondant-covered cupcakes have become increasingly popular and these sophisticated designs would grace the smartest party; they are suitable for bridal showers, wedding buffets, and adult birthdays. Use a light base such as the vanilla cake (page 83) or lime and coconut (page 80) without the buttercream as the fondant icing is very sweet.

you will need

2-inch round cakes

fondant icing—allow 2½ oz. per cake

pink and brown edible food colors

marzipan—allow 2 oz. per cake

2½-inch silver cupcake cases

ribbon or rubber bands to hold the cases in position

2 pastry bags

2 no. 1.5 tips

royal icing for the top design

method

1 Make the fondant icing (see page 144) and color half with pink and half with brown edible coloring. Cover the 2-inch round cakes first with marzipan and then colored fondant icing as shown in the techniques (pages 141 and 144). Place each fondant-covered cupcake in a silver case and hold in position with a tied length of plain ribbon or a rubber band until set.

2 Color some royal icing and fill a pastry bag with a no. 1.5 tip and the royal icing (use pink on brown cakes and vice versa). Using the template on page 153 as a guide, pipe the design freehand onto the top of each cupcake. Allow to set. Remove the ribbon or rubber band prior to serving.

monochrome lace

This design was inspired by lace from a Pearl Lowe collection. It is particularly striking in black and white and has become a firm favorite with clients of Little Venice Cake Company.

you will need

2-inch round cakes

marzipan—allow 2 oz. per cake

white rolled fondant—allow
2½ oz. per cake

black ribbon ⅜-inch wide—
allow 6 inches per cake

waxed paper

scribe

royal icing

black edible food color

pastry bag

no. 1.5 tip

method

1 Cover the 2-inch round cakes with marzipan and rolled fondant as shown in the techniques on pages 141 and 143. Fix a length of black ribbon around the base of each cake. Trace the template from page 156 onto waxed paper and, placing the tracing over each cake in turn, scribe the center flower and the middle of the ribbon bows onto the top of each cake using the scribe.

2 Color some royal icing with black edible coloring. Fill a pastry bag with a no. 1.5 tip and the black icing. Pipe the detail onto the cake as shown, adding the pearls underneath the scrolls and around the base ribbon.

tip

This design transposes well in a variety of colors—change the colors to complement your party.

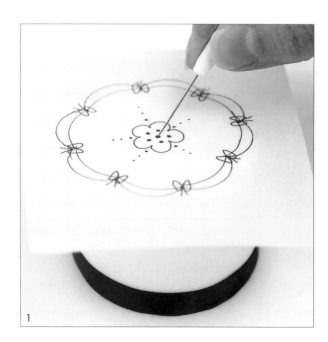

bollywood

These stylish Bollywood designs are bold, bright, and very up to date—and such fun. The vibrant colors of saffron, lime, tangerine, and fuchsia look particularly effective when they are clustered en masse.

you will need

2-inch round cakes

marzipan—allow 2 oz. per cake

yellow, orange, fuchsia, and lime colored rolled fondant—allow 2¹/₂ oz. per cake

gold ribbon ³/₈-inch wide—allow 6 inches per cake

waxed paper

scribe

royal icing

old-gold edible food color

pastry bag

no. 1.5 tip

gold dust

dipping alcohol

fine paintbrush

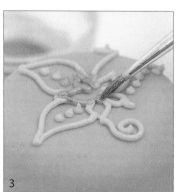

method

1 Cover the 2-inch round cakes with marzipan and colored rolled fondant as shown in the techniques on pages 141 and 143. Fix a length of gold ribbon around the base of each cake. Trace the two templates from page 152 onto waxed paper. Scribe one of the two designs onto the top of each cake using the scribe and the traced template.

2 Color some royal icing with old-gold food coloring. Fill a pastry bag with a no. 1.5 tip and old-gold royal icing. Pipe the detail onto each cake as shown, adding the pearls, swirls, and flowers. Allow to set for at least 2 hours.

3 Dissolve a small amount of gold dust in dipping alcohol and brush onto the Bollywood design using a fine paintbrush.

pretty posies

Delicately hand-piped flowers and leaves are very effective decoration for these little cakes. They look particularly impressive in all-white for weddings; I recreated this design in shades of pink on a larger cake for my goddaughter Imogen's christening.

you will need

2-inch round cakes

marzipan—allow 2 oz. per cake

ivory rolled fondant—allow 2½ oz. per cake

sage green ribbon ⅝-inch wide—allow 6 inches per cake

royal icing

purple, pink, and green edible food colors

3 pastry bags

2 no. 1.5 tips

method

1 Cover the 2-inch round cakes with marzipan and rolled fondant as shown in the techniques on pages 141 and 143. Fix a length of sage green ribbon around the base of each cake. Color some royal icing with the three edible food colors. Fill a pastry bag with no. 1.5 tip and purple royal icing. Pipe a circle of petals on the cake—trailing the petal to the center of each flower. Repeat over the top and sides of the cake in different sizes as shown.

2 Fill a second pastry bag with no. 1.5 tip and pink royal icing. Pipe a second row of petals inside the first coming to a point in the center of each flower.

3 Fill a third pastry bag with green royal icing and snip the end of the bag to form a small "V" (as shown in techniques for fondant red roses on page 41). Pressure pipe green leaves to frame the flowers as shown.

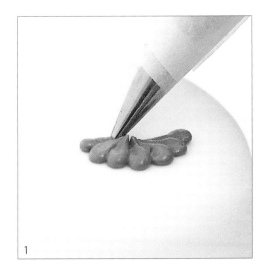

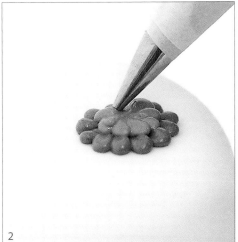

coconut butterflies

I made these coconut rounds out of the lime and coconut cake (page 80) but other flavors would work equally well. The sugar disks can be made in advance and you can use any colors to suit the celebration. These pretty little cakes are just right for a female birthday party.

you will need

2-inch round rolled fondant disks—allow ½ oz. per cake

confectioners' sugar, for dusting

waxed paper

scribe

3 pastry bags

no. 1.5, no. 2, and large star tips

royal icing for piping and flooding the butterflies

edible food colors of your choice

paintbrush

2-inch round cakes

metal spatula

buttercream—choose from vanilla, orange, lemon curd, and chocolate flavors (pages 138–9)—allow 1 oz. per cake

toasted coconut—allow ½ oz. per cake

method

1 Prepare the icing disks: roll out the white rolled fondant to a depth of ⅛ inch and stamp out 2-inch rounds. Place on a board or tray well dusted with confectioners' sugar and allow to dry overnight. Trace the butterfly template on page 152 onto waxed paper and scribe this onto each of the sugar disks. Fill a pastry bag with a no. 2 tip and colored royal icing. Pipe the outline of the butterfly as shown. Fill a separate pastry bag with another colored flooding icing and snip the end. Flood the wings of the butterflies as shown.

2 Use a paintbrush to carefully pull the icing to all corners of the wings. Allow to skin over for 20 minutes before decorating.

3 Fill a pastry bag with a no. 1.5 tip and the original colored royal icing. Pipe a 5-pointed flower on the top of both wings of each butterfly and 4 pearls on the lower wings. Allow to set overnight or at least 6 hours.

4 Cut out the individual round cakes—it helps if the cake is chilled for 30 minutes—and use a metal spatula to smooth a small amount of buttercream over the sides. Roll the cakes in the toasted coconut and set aside.

5 Fill a pastry bag with a large star tip and fresh buttercream. Pipe a swirl of buttercream on the top of each cake and position a sugar butterfly disk at an angle on the top. Present the cakes together on a pretty cake stand.

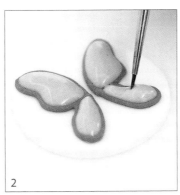

bugs and butterflies

These elaborate individually hand-painted cakes would look stunning individually boxed and ribboned and presented as wedding favors. The colors can be changed to suit any occasion. The technique is quite time consuming, so use a cake base with a good shelf life—such as the sticky date (page 86) or banana butterscotch cake (page 85).

you will need

2-inch round cakes

marzipan—allow 2 oz. per cake

caramel rolled fondant—allow 2½ oz. per cake

berry-colored ribbon ⅝-inch wide—allow 6 inches per cake

royal icing to fix ribbon in position

waxed paper

scribe

cocoa butter

various color dusts

paintbrushes

method

1 Cover the 2-inch round cakes with marzipan and rolled fondant as shown in the techniques on pages 141 and 143. Fix a length of berry-colored ribbon around the base of each cake with a little royal icing. Trace a range of designs from the templates on page 152 onto waxed paper. Scribe these onto the cakes using a scribe. Use different bugs and butterflies in different positions for a truly individual collection.

2 Melt a small piece of cocoa butter on a small saucer over a cup of hot water. Blend the cocoa butter with a color dust and paint the traced designs onto each cake. Build up the color and intensity by adding more layers. Finish by adding fine black detail to each bug for their limbs, antennae, and pincers.

tip

If the cocoa butter starts to solidify, replace the water in the cup underneath the saucer with freshly boiled water.

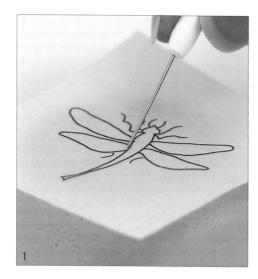

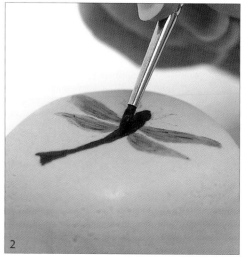

christmas canapé collection

When we invite our neighbors in for champagne and festive treats at Christmas, these chic cakes are perfect—hand decorated with seasonal designs and brushed with gold—and boxed they make a lovely gift. I would recommend the chocolate and almond (page 90), sticky date (page 86), or chocca mocca pecan cake (page 95) for inclusion inside.

you will need

2-inch square cakes

white chocolate plastique—allow 2½ oz. per cake

dark chocolate plastique—allow 3 oz. per cake

gum paste colored with old gold—allow 5g for 3 holly leaves for 1 cake

small rolling pin

small holly veiner/plunger-cutter (¾ inch)

new kitchen sponge

1 quantity royal icing (page 145)

old-gold edible food color

gold ribbon ⅝-inch wide—allow 8 inches per cake

waxed paper

scribe

pastry bag

no. 1.5 tip

gold luster

dipping alcohol

fine paintbrush

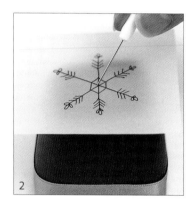

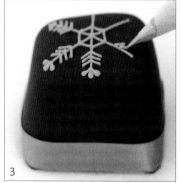

method

1 Cover each 2-inch square cake with an initial covering of white chocolate plastique followed by a top coat of dark chocolate plastique as shown in the techniques on page 149. Roll out the colored gum paste (page 141) very finely and vein and cut out holly leaves. Allow to dry on a soft sponge to create interesting shapes.

2 Color the royal icing with old-gold coloring. Fix a length of gold ribbon around the base of each cake with a little royal icing. Trace the snowflake design on page 154 onto waxed paper and scribe the design through onto the top of one cake. Repeat with one third the total number of cakes.

3 Fill a pastry bag with a no. 1.5 tip and old-gold royal icing. Hand pipe the snowflake design following the template. Hand pipe random Christmas trees on the sides of another third of the cakes as shown. Place 3 holly leaves on the top of each of the remaining cakes and hand pipe berries in the center.

4 Suspend a small amount of gold luster in dipping alcohol in a small bowl. Brush the gold luster liquid carefully over the designs, ensuring the holly leaves are well covered and painting in stars at the top of some of the Christmas trees. Present on a gold plate or Christmas platter or in clear boxes tied with gold ribbon.

polka swirl hearts

These bright, vibrant cakes look stunning on a tiered cake stand. Change the colors to suit the occasion. They were originally commissioned for a Valentine's Day promotion held at London's famous Fortnum & Mason but have now become a firm favorite at Little Venice Cake Company.

you will need

2-inch square cakes

marzipan—allow 2½ oz. per cake

white rolled fondant—allow 3 oz. per cake

party ribbon ⅜-inch wide— allow 8 inches per cake

royal icing

small rolling pin

various colored rolled fondants

heart plunger-cutter

sugar glue

edible food color of choice

pastry bag

no. 1.5 tip

method

1 Cover the cakes with marzipan and rolled fondant following the method given in techniques (pages 141 and 143). Fix a length of ⅜-inch ribbon around the base of each cake with a little royal icing.

2 Roll out the colored rolled fondants very finely to a thickness of ¹⁄₁₂–⅛ inch. Press the outside of the heart cutter firmly to cut out the shape. Carefully lift the paste and depress the center of the cutter (which is usually spring-loaded) to release the cut-out heart.

3 Randomly fix the hearts onto the cakes using sugar glue, allowing 7–8 per cake.

4 Color some royal icing for the swirls. Fit the pastry bag with the no. 1.5 tip and fill with the colored royal icing. Pipe swirls onto a selection of the hearts, starting at the inside of the heart and working your way outward. Allow to set for at least 6 hours before serving or packaging.

chocolate cups

These chocolate cups are perfect served as individual desserts for a dinner party or summer occasion. Each cup is surrounded with a chocolate collar and filled with fresh berries.

you will need

2-inch round cakes

white chocolate plastique—
allow 4½ oz. per cake plus
2½ oz. for the collars

confectioners' sugar, for dusting

small rolling pin

pastry brush

brandy or cooled boiled water

cream grosgrain ribbon ⅝-inch
wide—allow 8 inches per cake

small quantity royal icing

seasonal berries—raspberries,
red currants, strawberries—
allow 1½ oz. per cake

method

1 Cover each cake with an initial covering of white chocolate plastique, as shown in techniques page 149. Lightly dust a clean work surface with confectioners' sugar. Roll out a 2½ oz. piece of white chocolate plastique to a rectangle measuring approximately 8 x 1 inches. Trim the base edge with a sharp knife and feather the top edge using a small nonstick rolling pin.

2 Brush around the side of the cakes with brandy or cooled boiled water and wrap the collar around as shown. Use a sharp knife to trim the chocolate plastique so the two edges join.

3 Fix a length of cream grosgrain ribbon around the base of the cake with royal icing or melted chocolate and fill the cup with seasonal berries.

tip

Substitute dark chocolate for the white chocolate or have a combination of the two for a larger social gathering.

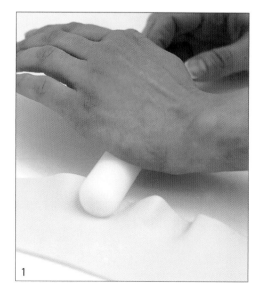

tricolor chocolate rose

Individually covered and decorated chocolate cakes make a fabulous gift presented together in a box. These cakes are perennially popular with clients of Little Venice Cake Company. They are often chosen as wedding cakes to be served for dessert: a perfectly presented chocolate cake for every guest.

you will need

2-inch round cakes

white , milk, or dark chocolate plastique for the roses—allow ¼ oz. each per rose and leaves

plastic wrap

metal spatula

white chocolate plastique for first coat—allow 2 oz. per cake

white, milk, or dark chocolate plastique for top coat—allow 2½ oz. per cake

pastry bag

melted chocolate

grosgrain ribbon ⅝-inch wide— allow 6 inches per cake

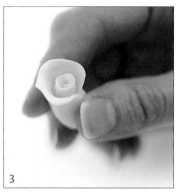

method

1 Make the roses. Warm a small amount of chocolate plastique between your palms and roll into a ball. Place between 2 sheets of plastic. Flatten quickly with the base of your palm, then, using your index finger, flatten two-thirds of the way round the ball, leaving a thicker base.

2 Remove the chocolate from the plastic wrap and, holding the thicker base, gently roll the chocolate to form the center of the rose.

3 Repeat step 1 to create 2 more petals. Wrap a petal around the rose center, then fix the final petal so they overlap one another. Gently tease the petals into shape. Slice the base off the rose using a metal spatula.

4 Allow for 3 roses and 3 leaves per cake. To make the leaves roll a small ball of dark chocolate plastique into a sausage approximately ¾-inch long and flatten into shape. Pinch the long sides together to form a leaf shape. Set aside to firm.

5 Cover the 2-inch round cake with an initial coat of white chocolate plastique followed with a top coat as shown in the techniques, page 149. Fill a pastry bag with a little melted chocolate and use to fix a length of grosgrain ribbon around the base of each cake and 3 roses and 3 leaves on top of each cake.

champagne primroses

This fresh design combines spring sugar primroses with delicately hand-piped champagne pearls. It would work particularly well with the light, fruity flavored cakes—lime and coconut (page 80), banana butterscotch (page 85), or vanilla cake (page 83) with lemon curd buttercream (page 138), for all special occasions or summer picnics.

you will need

2-inch round cakes

yellow gum paste—allow ¾ oz. per cake (3 primroses)

1-inch primrose cutter

pale green dust

dipping alcohol

fine paintbrush

marzipan—allow 2 oz. per cake

white rolled fondant—allow 2½ oz. per cake

yellow ribbon ⅜-inch wide— allow 6 inches per cake

white royal icing

pastry bag

no. 1.5 tip

method

1 To make the primroses, mold a marble-sized ball of yellow gum paste into a "Mexican hat"—pinching and slightly hollowing the end as shown.

2 Place the "hat" face down and fit the primrose cutter over the back and press down firmly and evenly on both sides of the cutter. Remove the excess paste. Pinch each petal carefully to thin the petals further.

3 Dissolve a little green dust in dipping alcohol and with a fine paintbrush paint the center of the primrose as shown. Repeat for 3 primroses per cake and leave to dry and firm.

4 Cover each 2-inch round cake with marzipan and rolled fondant as shown in the techniques, pages 141 and 143. Fix a length of yellow ribbon around the base of each cake with a little royal icing.

5 Fill a pastry bag with no. 1.5 tip and white royal icing. Pipe a cascade of pearls onto the cake at random intervals as shown. Fix the primroses on top with a dab of royal icing.

tip

For more variation make a variety of flowers and change the ribbons to complement.

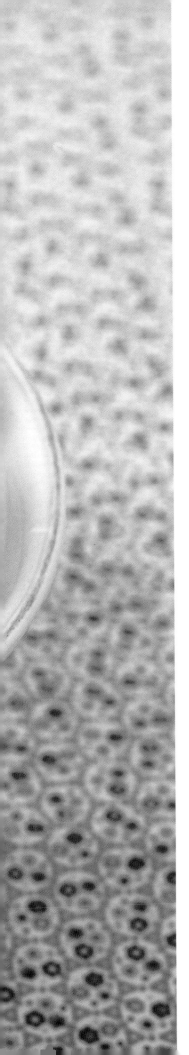

fondant red roses

These fondant cakes look very effective en masse. They have a sugar-molded red rose in the center of each cake framed by three hand-piped green leaves. They work well with the lime and coconut cake (page 80, without the buttercream) or the vanilla cake (page 83) with added lemon or orange zest.

you will need

2-inch round cakes

red rolled fondant—allow 1 oz. per rose

marzipan—allow 2 oz. per cake

fondant icing—allow 2½ oz. per cake

2½-inch silver cupcake cases

ribbon or rubber bands to hold the cases in position

royal icing for the leaves

green edible food color

pastry bag

method

1 Use the red rolled fondant to make the sugar molded roses (see page 36) but make a center and 4 more petals.

2 Cover the 2-inch round cakes with marzipan and fondant icing as shown in the techniques, pages 141 and 144. Place each fondant-covered cupcake in a silver case and hold in position with a tied length of plain ribbon or an rubber band until set.

3 Color the royal icing with green food coloring. Fill a pastry bag with the green royal icing and snip the end diagonally in both directions to form a "V" as shown.

4 Holding the pastry bag at the center of the cupcake, pressure pipe 3 leaves tapering out towards the edge of the cake. Carefully position a sugar-molded red rose into the center and allow to set. Remove the ribbon or rubber band prior to serving.

apple-blossom bears

Baby showers are always popular and are a lovely occasion to celebrate the impending arrival of a newborn baby. These gorgeous cakes would make the perfect accompaniment or could be mailed out as a birth announcement cake. Alternatively, they could celebrate a baby's christening or first birthday. I think these cakes work especially well with our lime and coconut cake (page 80).

you will need

2-inch square cakes

modeling paste—allow 1 oz. per cake

teddy bear brown, light brown, black, blue, and apple-green edible food colors

modeling tools/wooden pick

sugar glue

white royal icing

pastry bags

2 no. 1.5 tips

very fine paintbrush

small rolling pin

white rolled fondant—allow 3 oz. per cake including the apple-blossom flowers

small (⅛ inch) and medium (¼ inch) flower plunger-cutters

marzipan—allow 2½ oz. per cake

white ribbon ⅝-inch wide and apple-green ribbon ¼-inch wide—allow 8 inches each per cake

method

1 Make the teddy bears. Remove sufficient modeling paste to make the lighter brown muzzle and black nose and color accordingly. Color the remainder of the paste teddy-bear brown. Draw a 2½-inch square as a template and mold the paste into the body parts of the teddy bear as shown—ensuring the finished bear will fit inside the 2½-inch square template. Fix together with sugar glue, pipe the eyes with colored royal icing—white, blue with a black pupil, and paint the mouth with black food coloring.

2 Roll a small amount of white fondant out thinly and plunge-cut the apple blossom flowers in two sizes. Allow to dry on a piece of tissue.

3 Cover the 2-inch square cakes with marzipan and rolled fondant as shown in techniques, pages 141 and 143. Fix a length of ⅝-inch white ribbon overlaid with ¼-inch apple-green ribbon around the base of each cake with a little royal icing. Using a pastry bag filled with no. 1.5 tip and white royal icing, fix a garland of apple-blossom flowers onto each cake as shown, concentrating on either the top corner or base corner for each cake. Pipe a white pearl into the center of each flower. Fill another pastry bag with pale apple-green icing and a no. 1.5 tip and pipe tiny leaves between the flowers to finish.

4 Fix the teddy bears onto the top of some of the cakes with a dab of royal icing.

on the farm

These animal cakes are cute enough to bring out the child in all of us! I made these for an Easter charity morning at my son's school and also supplied them exclusively to Harvey Nichols' store in London for an Easter promotion. They make a lovely take-home gift for a child's birthday party—simply wrapped in a cotton napkin or individually boxed. Choose a cake that will appeal to children such as vanilla (page 83), chocolate and almond (page 90), or lime and coconut (page 80).

you will need

2-inch square cakes

marzipan—allow 2½ oz. per cake

white rolled fondant—allow 3 oz. per cake

party ribbon ⅜-inch wide

royal icing

yellow, orange, brown, green, pink, black, and white rolled fondant for the animals

modeling tools/wooden pick

sugar glue

method

1 Cover the 2-inch square cakes with marzipan and rolled fondant as shown in the techniques, pages 141 and 143. Fix a length of ⅜-inch ribbon around the base of each cake with a little royal icing.

2 Make the animals—fixing everything in position with sugar glue. For the duck, mold an oval piece of yellow fondant to form the head. Add the orange beak, eyes, and yellow cowlick at the top.

3 For the sheep, mold an oval piece of brown fondant and use a knife to create a mouth. Add the eyes, 2 floppy ears, and white balls of fondant for the wool. Finish with green fondant to resemble chewing grass.

4 For the pig start with a round piece of pink fondant and flatten. Add the snout and use a marking tool to create the nostrils. Finish with the eyes and 2 ears.

5 Fix the animals onto the top of each cake with a dab of royal icing.

small
party cakes

small party cakes These are both stylish and elegant—showcasing a larger single tiered or multi-tiered cake creates drama, excitement, and a real sense of occasion. They suit a more formal celebration as these cakes will create a natural photograph opportunity when gathering all the guests together for a champagne toast. I have presented a collection of my favorites in this chapter for weddings, anniversaries, birthdays, christenings, as well as some fabulous Christmas cakes. These designs can be constructed from the cakes in the chapter *Delicious Treats*.

cherry blossom

There is a saying that a life spent searching for the perfect cherry blossom is a life well spent. Here is a perfect cherry-blossom cake—combining soft brown and pink colors on two tiers. I have used the sticky date cake (page 86) as the base, but do please choose your favorite!

you will need

2-inch and 3-inch round cakes cut from an 8-inch square cake

5 oz. marzipan

1 lb. ivory rolled fondant

5-inch round cake board

waxed paper

scribe

white royal icing

chocolate brown, dark pink, and pale pink edible food colors

16 inches pale pink ribbon $\frac{1}{4}$-inch wide, for the cakes

24 inches chocolate brown ribbon $\frac{1}{8}$-inch wide, for the cakes and bow

3 pastry bags

3 no. 1.5 tips

16 inches dusky pink ribbon $\frac{5}{8}$-inch wide, for the board

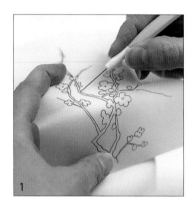 

method

1 Cover the two round cakes with marzipan and rolled fondant following the method given in techniques, pages 141 and 143, then stack centrally on a 5-inch round cake board covered with ivory fondant.

2 Trace the cherry blossom design (page 153) onto a sheet of waxed or tracing paper and scribe onto the base and top tier of the cake. Color one third of the royal icing with chocolate brown food coloring, one third with pink, and one third a paler pink.

3 Fix a length of pink ribbon overlaid with brown ribbon around the base of each tier with a little royal icing. Tie a bow with a piece of brown ribbon and fix to the ribbon on the top tier, over the join, with a little royal icing. Fill 3 pastry bags fitted with no. 1.5 tips with the different colored royal icing. Beginning with the brown icing, pressure pipe the branches following the scribed design. With the pink icing, pipe pearls to make the cherry blossom, adding either a paler or darker pink center for authenticity. Fix the $\frac{5}{8}$-inch ribbon round the cake board with a little royal icing.

little venice lace™

I designed this cake with London's famous Dorchester Hotel as the inspiration. The vintage hand-piped lace and pearl design is brushed with a pearlized luster for a very special formal occasion such as an intimate wedding, wedding anniversary, or engagement. The pattern can be traced and used on a larger tiered wedding cake for a more social gathering. This lace has become the iconic trademark of Little Venice Cake Company.

you will need

8-inch square cake

1 lb. 5oz. marzipan

1 lb. 10 oz. ivory rolled fondant

waxed paper

scribe

pastry bag

no. 2 tips

white royal icing

24 inches ivory ribbon ³⁄₈-inch wide

topaz luster

dipping alcohol

fine paintbrush

3 hand-molded ivory roses and 8 rose leaves to decorate

method

1 Cut out a 6-inch heart from the square cake. Following the techniques on pages 140 and 142, cover the heart with marzipan and fondant. Trace the lace design (page 154) onto a piece of tracing or waxed paper and position around the cake, ensuring the center of one repeat is lined up with the point of the heart. Scribe the design onto the cake.

2 Fill a pastry bag with a no. 2 tip and white royal icing. Fix a length of ribbon around the base of the cake with a little royal icing, then pressure pipe the design around the sides of the cake as shown. Allow to set for at least 4 hours.

3 Suspend a small amount (½ tsp) topaz luster in dipping alcohol. Using a fine paintbrush, paint the luster onto the entire design as shown. Dress the cake with lustered hand-molded roses (page 36) and green rose leaves or a small corsage of fresh flowers tied with organza ribbon.

charleston pearls

This cake has been inspired by the 1920s Charleston pearls—endless strings of pearls worn in varying lengths and widths along with the traditional flapper dresses and feathers. This is a very bold design that transposes well onto a larger multi-tiered wedding cake or, as here, for an intimate wedding, dressed with fresh roses studded with crystals.

you will need

3-inch and 5-inch square cakes cut from an 8-inch square cake

1 lb. 14 oz. marzipan

2 lb. 4 oz. white rolled fondant

thin card

scribe

pastry bag

no. 3 tip

white royal icing

1 yard white ribbon ⅝-inch wide

paintbrush

clear edible gel

7 small-headed white roses tied with white organza ribbon

12 clear crystals ½-inch diameter

12 white wires gauge 28

method

1 Following the techniques on page 140 and 142, cover the 3-inch and 5-inch square cakes with marzipan and rolled fondant and stack centrally. Trace the 3 templates from page 153 onto thin card and cut out. Scribe the different curves around the top edge of each tier, overlapping the designs as you work your way around.

2 Fill a pastry bag with no. 3 tip and white royal icing. Fix a length of white ribbon around the base of each tier then begin piping the strands of pearls—making each slightly different—pressure piping different intensities as shown. Allow to set for at least 4 hours.

3 Using a paintbrush, brush each pearl with clear edible gel. To finish, hand tie a small bouquet of fresh white roses with a length of white organza ribbon and bow. Thread crystals onto white wires gauge 28 and twist to secure. Trim the end of the wire to 1-inch length and insert one crystal into the center of each rose, and some between.

polka passion

Bright and vibrant, this pretty cake design was adopted by Harrods store in Knightsbridge, London—with a showgirl leaping out of the top of a 3-tier version! I have worked with pink and green colors, but adapt these to complement your own theme. This design works equally well on a single tier or little individual cakes.

you will need

2-inch and 3-inch round cakes cut from an 8-inch square cake

5 oz. marzipan

1 lb. 2 oz. white rolled fondant

5-inch round cake board

leaf green, pale pink, and darker pink edible food colors

white royal icing

confectioners' sugar, for dusting

small rolling pin

polka dot plunger-cutter ½-inch diameter

sugar glue

3 pastry bags

3 no. 1.5 tips

16 inches pretty ribbon ³⁄₈-inch wide, for the cakes

16 inches fuchsia pink ribbon ⁵⁄₈-inch wide, for the board

method

1 Following the techniques on page 141 and 143, cover the 2-inch and 3-inch round cakes with marzipan and rolled fondant and stack centrally on a 5-inch round cake board covered with white fondant.

2 Divide the remaining fondant equally into three and color each with green, pale or darker pink. Divide the royal icing into 3 bowls and color each with green, pale or darker pink to match the fondant. Lightly dust a work surface with confectioners' sugar and roll out the 3 fondant colors. Plunge cut polka dots and use sugar glue to fix these into position on the cake randomly—ensuring the colors are well interspersed and there is space between the polka dots.

3 Fill 3 pastry bags with no. 1.5 tips and the colored royal icing in each. Fix a length of pretty ribbon around the base of each cake and pressure pipe pearls around the edge of each polka dot as shown—leaving sufficient space to pipe a second row. With a second color, pipe elongated pearls between the first as shown. Finally, fix the pink ribbon around the cake board with a dab of royal icing.

metallic painted irises

Metallic lusters paint well onto smooth, dark chocolate. The effect
is quite art nouveau and here I have painted a collection of iris flowers
and butterflies using copper, dark bronze, and gold lusters. This
technique is quite expressive allowing you to be a free-flowing artist!

you will need

3-inch and 4-inch square cakes
cut from an 8-inch square cake

1 lb. 5 oz. white chocolate
plastique

1 lb. 14 oz. dark chocolate
plastique covering

6-inch square cake board

1 yard dark brown grosgrain
ribbon ⅝-inch wide

waxed paper

scribe

bronze, copper, and gold
metallic lusters

dipping alcohol

paintbrushes

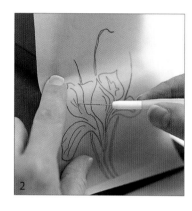

method

1 Following the technique on page 149, cover the 3-inch and 4-inch square
cakes with an initial coat of white chocolate plastique with a top coat of dark
chocolate plastique covering, and stack offset on a 6-inch square cake board
covered with dark chocolate plastique. Fix a length of grosgrain ribbon
around each cake and the base board.

2 Trace the flower and butterfly designs from page 156 onto waxed
or tracing paper.

3 Use a scribe to transfer the design onto the cake, decorating the sides
and the top of the cake.

4 Suspend the separate colored metallic lusters in dipping alcohol and
paint the iris design and butterflies. Build up the layers to create depth
of color.

tip
This technique also works well on individual chocolate-covered cakes.

cannes-cannes

Inspired by the catwalk fashions of the famous designer Chanel, this cake is the epitome of French elegance—Parisian chic and Cannes glamour! It works well in different color combinations, but I love the classic and sophisticated black and white look.

you will need

2-inch and 4-inch square cakes cut from an 8-inch square cake

1 lb. marzipan

2 lb. 4 oz. white rolled fondant

4-inch square cake board

9 oz. gum paste

small rolling pin

brandy, for brushing

confectioner's sugar, for dusting

pastry brush

cooled boiled water or sugar glue

1 yard black ribbon ³⁄₈-inch wide

royal icing to fix the ribbon

decorated cake stand (optional)

method

1 Following the technique on page 141 and 143 cover the 2-inch and 4-inch square cakes with marzipan and fondant and stack centrally on the cake board. Blend the remaining white fondant with the gum paste—this will allow the paste to set firmer and hold its position. Lightly knead the paste then roll out to a collar length 20 x 3¹⁄₂ inches. Trim with a sharp knife then feather the upper edge of the collar with the small rolling pin.

2 Brush the sides of the base tier with brandy and fix the collar into position. Trim with a sharp knife to form a neat join at the back. Repeat with the top tier making a smaller collar, dimensions approximately 10 x 3¹⁄₂ inches, and applying as before.

3 Dust the work surface with a little confectioners' sugar. Roll out lengths of paste 6 x 1¹⁄₄ inches and feather the top edge. Gather the frills up as shown.

4 Brush the inside of the collar with cooled boiled water or sugar glue and fix the frills inside the collars. Repeat until the collars are completely filled with frills and allow to firm. Remove any excess confectioners' sugar from the frills using a dry pastry brush.

5 Make 2 black ribbon bows. Fix a length of ribbon around each tier with royal icing at the back of the cake and finish with a ribbon bow on the front corner. Serve on a decorated cake stand, if you like.

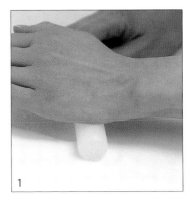

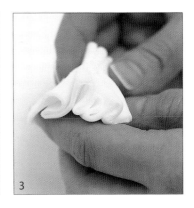

cascading roses and lilies

I have used alternate tiers of white and dark chocolate, tumbling with a cascade of hand-molded white and dark chocolate roses, lilies, and leaves to create this contemporary chocolate design. Chocolate will complement any chocolate base cake, or opt for a light vanilla base with vanilla, chocolate, or espresso buttercream.

you will need

2-inch and 3-inch round cakes cut from an 8-inch square cake

1 lb. 5 oz. white chocolate plastique to cover and for the flowers

7 oz. dark chocolate plastique for the flowers

ball modeling tool

small rolling pin

¾-inch rose veiner and cutter

1 lb. 2 oz. dark chocolate plastique covering

5-inch round cake board

8 inches cream grosgrain ribbon ⅝-inch wide

30 inches dark brown grosgrain ribbon ⅝-inch wide

2 pastry bags

2 oz. white chocolate, melted

2 oz. dark chocolate, melted

method

1 Make the flowers: roses, lilies, and leaves. The exact number you will require will depend on the size of the flowers, the size of the tiers, and how much of the cake you want to cover. For this cake I made 10 white chocolate roses, 5 lilies, 5 leaves; 6 dark chocolate roses, 3 lilies, and 5 leaves. Follow the technique on page 36 for the roses, making a center and 4 more petals.

2 For the arum lilies, roll a pea-sized piece of paste into a sausage approximately 1 inch long. Cut a triangular piece of paste and using a ball tool, thin out the edges.

3 Wrap this around the sausage to create the lily. Roll the remaining paste out and use a rose cutter to vein and cut out the leaves.

4 Following the techniques on page 149, cover the 2-inch and 3-inch round cakes with an initial coat of white chocolate plastique with a top coat of either white or dark chocolate plastique and stack centrally on a 5-inch round cake board covered with dark chocolate plastique. Fix a length of grosgrain ribbon around each cake and the base board.

5 Fill 2 pastry bags, one with melted white chocolate and one with melted dark chocolate. Starting with the dark chocolate flowers, fix these into position on the lower tier, working from the base board upwards. As the flowers join the upper tier switch to white chocolate flowers and finish with a topiary flourish on the top tier.

tip

It is always worth making more flowers than you might need to make sure you have enough to make a fabulous, full garland. Any spare flowers will keep in an airtight container for 6 months.

For larger or more tiers, wrap a 1-inch thick sausage of paste from the top of the cake to the base board. This will act as a guide to follow when applying the flowers and also provide a good platform to adhere the flowers.

classic christmas rose

Christmas is a fabulous time of year for a celebration cake. I have included three Christmas cakes in this chapter—this design being the most traditional. You can modernize this cake by opting for a non-traditional flavor of cake inside such as the sticky date cake (page 86) or follow this design for your own favorite rich fruitcake recipe.

you will need

8-inch round cake

small rolling pin

2 oz. white gum paste

1-inch rose cutter

ball modeling tool

sugar glue

white royal icing

yellow and red edible food color

2 pastry bag

2 no. 1.5 tips

fine paintbrush

leaf-green color dust

2 lb. 4 oz. marzipan

2 lb. 12 oz. white rolled fondant

28 inches each red ribbon 1 inch wide, green ribbon ⁵⁄₈-inch wide, and white ribbon ¹⁄₄-inch wide

2¹⁄₂ oz. holly-green gum paste

1-inch holly veiner and plunger-cutter

aluminum foil

³⁄₄-inch holly veiner and plunger-cutter

method

1 Make 3 Christmas roses: roll out the white gum paste very thinly. Cut out 5 petals for each rose with the rose cutter. Use a ball modeling tool to thin the edges of the petal.

2 Lay 5 petals in a circle as shown, held in position with sugar glue. Pinch the tips of the rose petals. Color 1 tbsp of the royal icing with yellow food color. Fill a pastry bag with a no. 1.5 tip and yellow royal icing. Pipe the center of the rose as shown.

3 Brush the outer tips of the rose with green color dust as shown and leave to dry. Repeat to make the other roses.

4 Following the techniques on page 140 and 142, cover the round cake with marzipan and fondant. Starting with the widest ribbon (red), fix around the cake, overlaid with the green and finally white ribbon. Fix with a dab of royal icing.

5 Roll out the green gum paste and vein and plunge-cut six 1-inch holly leaves for the top of the cake. Position these on a scrunched piece of aluminum foil to firm in a textured position. Meanwhile vein and plunge-cut 20–25 ³⁄₄-inch green holly leaves. Position these around the side of the cake at a slight angle, fixed into position with white royal icing. Color 1 tbsp royal icing with red edible food color. Fill a pastry bag with a no. 1.5 tip and red royal icing. Pipe a single berry beneath each holly leaf around the cake. Fix the larger holly leaves and roses into position on the top of the cake with royal icing, and finish by piping the red berries on the top beside the holly.

tip

Gum paste dries out very quickly so only work on one rose at a time. Once the rose has been made, it will set firm within a couple of hours. Because it has a higher quantity of gum tragacanth, it can be rolled much thinner than fondant, creating more delicate flowers.

sugar candy

Our candy stripe design has become synonymous with Little Venice Cake Company. Here I have used various widths of colored fondant around two tiers of cake and added some hand-iced sugar butterflies—made a couple of days beforehand—for real party pizzazz.

you will need

2-inch and 4-inch round cakes cut from an 8-inch square cake

1 lb. 2 oz. marzipan

2 lb. 12 oz. white rolled fondant (color 9 oz. fuchsia pink for the board)

6-inch round cake board

fuchsia pink, buttercup yellow, tangerine orange, and leaf green edible food colors

scribe

small rolling pin

confectioners' sugar, for dusting

sugar glue

20 inches fuchsia pink ribbon ⅝-inch wide, for the board

for the butterflies

tracing and waxed paper

masking tape

edible food colors

no. 1.5 and no. 3 tips

pastry bags

white royal icing

fine paintbrush

wooden pick

method

1 Following the techniques on pages 141 and 143, cover the 2-inch and 4-inch round cakes with marzipan and white fondant and stack centrally on a 6-inch round cake board covered with fuchsia pink fondant.

2 Divide the remaining fondant equally into 4, and color each with fuchsia pink, buttercup yellow, tangerine orange, or leaf green to the desired intensity. Scribe around the top of each cake as a guideline. Roll out the fondant very finely on a work surface lightly dusted with confectioners' sugar. Cut the paste into strips of varying widths. Don't prepare too many in advance as the paste will dry out. Cover any prepared strips with plastic wrap.

3 Use the sugar glue to fix the strips into position around the sides of each tier of the cake as shown, making sure the strip butts up to the preceding strip. Trim the end of each strip to your scribed guideline with a sharp knife.

4 Finish with 5 hand-made iced butterflies made using the run-out method as shown in the techniques on page 145. Fix the pink ribbon round the board with a small quantity of royal icing.

sleeping polar bear

This polar bear reminds me of my son George—he looks so angelic when fast asleep. I have domed the top of the cake and laid a sheet of white fondant over a blue iced cake to resemble an iceberg. With the holly and berries on top of his head he looks as though he has filled his tummy with a hearty Christmas lunch—just as it should be!

you will need

6-inch round cake plus extra cake to add a dome on the top (all cut from an 8-inch cake)

buttercream or apricot jam

1 lb. 4 oz. blue rolled fondant

1 lb. 10 oz. marzipan

9-inch round cake board

48 inches blue ribbon ⅝-inch wide

small rolling pin

1 lb. 2 oz. white rolled fondant

sharp knife

brandy or cooled boiled water

pastry brush

modeling tools

fine paintbrush

black, holly green, and red edible food colors

holly leaf veiner and plunger-cutter

craft knife

sugar glue

white royal icing

pastry bag

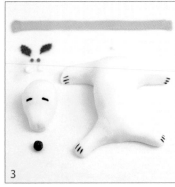

method

1 Cut out a 6-inch round cake and pack extra cake on top to create a dome shape. Use buttercream or apricot jam to hold in place. Reserve a small quantity of blue fondant for the scarf. Following the techniques on pages 140 and 142, cover the cake with marzipan and blue fondant and place on a 9-inch round cake board covered with blue fondant. Fix a length of ribbon around the base of the cake and the cake board.

2 Roll out 7 oz. white fondant to approximately 6-inch round. Cut the outline with a sharp knife. Brush the top of the cake with brandy or cooled boiled water and lay the white fondant over the top of the cake.

3 Make the polar bear: mold white fondant into a body with 4 legs; a head, small tail, and 2 ears. Paint the toes with black edible color and a fine paintbrush. Color a little fondant black and make a nose and 2 eyes.

4 Color some fondant green and cut out 2 holly leaves; color a little fondant red and make berries. Using the reserved blue fondant, roll out to create a scarf. Cut the ends with a fine craft knife to make a fringe. While the fondant is still malleable construct the polar bear directly onto the cake so it molds to the shape—use sugar glue to hold the pieces together. Wrap the scarf around the head before fixing into position. Place a small amount of white royal icing in a pastry bag, and use to fix the holly and berries into position.

bunny alphabet block

This cake is inspired by a child's alphabet block. I have made the cake very deep to create a cube—stack three layers of cake with two layers of buttercream before covering with marzipan and fondant. You can change the color of the icing for a special little girl or boy, or make three cakes of different sizes and have a trio of alphabet blocks.

you will need

4-inch cube cake (cut out from a 8-inch square cake)

1 lb. 5oz. marzipan

2 lb. 4oz. yellow rolled fondant

6-inch square cake board

20 inches white ribbon ³⁄₈-inch wide, for the cake

26 inches white ribbon ⁵⁄₈-inch wide, for the board

white royal icing

9 oz. white rolled fondant for the bunny

modeling tools

black and pink edible food colors, for the nose and eyes

sugar glue

small rolling pin

7 oz. white rolled fondant for the panels

tracing or waxed paper

2 oz. yellow gum paste, for the letters

scalpel

method

1 Following the techniques on pages 140 and 142, cover the cube cake with marzipan and yellow fondant and place on a 6-inch square cake board covered with yellow fondant. Fix a length of ribbon around the base of the cake and the cake board with a little royal icing.

2 Make the bunny: mold the white fondant into a body, head, ears, tail, jowls, eyes, and teeth. Color a small amount into black for the eyes and pink for the nose. While the fondant is still malleable, construct the bunny directly onto the cake so it molds to the shape—use sugar glue to hold the components together.

3 Roll out the white fondant for the panels and cut into 5 panels each 2¹⁄₂ inches square. Fix these into position on the sides and top of the cake with sugar glue. Trace and cut out the alphabet letters from page 152. Roll out the yellow gum paste very thinly and use a scalpel to cut out each letter.

4 Position one letter on each of the 4 sides of the cake (you don't need one for the top) and fix into position with sugar glue.

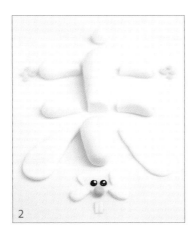

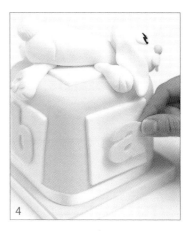

elephant polka dot

I love the way this elephant is clambering up and over the edge of the cake. This charming design is perfect for a child's birthday party. You could make smaller elephant heads and use them on the top of individual cakes, or a family of these whole elephants climbing over a tiered cake for a larger party.

you will need

8-inch oval cake (bake in an oval pan or cut out from a square cake)

1 lb. 12 oz. marzipan

2 lb. 14 oz. white rolled fondant

11-inch oval cake board

60 inches blue ribbon ⁵⁄₈-inch wide

white royal icing

9 oz. gray rolled fondant

modeling tools

sugar glue

shades of blue and black edible food colors

pastry bags

no. 1.5 tips

small rolling pin

⁵⁄₈-inch, ³⁄₄-inch, and 1¹⁄₄-inch circle cutters

method

1 Following the techniques on pages 140 and 142, cover the oval cake with marzipan and fondant and place on an 11-inch oval cake board covered with white fondant. Fix a length of ribbon around both the base of the cake and the cake board with a little royal icing.

2 Make the elephant: mold the gray fondant into a body, head with trunk, 4 legs, 2 ears, eyelids, and trunk end. Mold white feet pads and toes, tusks, and white eyes. While the fondant is still malleable, construct the elephant onto the cake so it molds to the shape; use sugar glue to hold the pieces together. Color a small amount of royal icing black, and pipe the eye pupils.

3 Divide the remainder of the fondant into 3 and color one third pale blue, one third dark blue, and keep one third white. Roll out the colored fondant very finely to a thickness of about ¹⁄₁₂ inch. Press the outside of the cutter firmly to cut out the shapes. Carefully lift the fondant and depress the center, which is usually spring loaded to release the cut-out shape. Cut out circles of all 3 colors and fix onto the cake with sugar glue.

4 Fill pastry bags with no. 1.5 tips and white, pale blue, or navy royal icing. Pipe a swirl on some of the circles starting in the center and working outward.

santa star

I was inspired by a Christmas-star decoration that Santa left for each of my sons in their stockings last year! This is a simple design that can be made with children for a very effective Christmas cake; all the components are cut out using the templates and built up in three layers. Make the pieces well in advance and decorate a cake on the run up to Christmas. Make a number of these for great gifts!

you will need

6-inch round cake

1 lb. 5 oz. marzipan

3 lb. 5 oz. white rolled fondant to cover the cake and board

9-inch round cake board

20 inches red ribbon ⅝-inch wide

1 yard red ribbon 1¼-inch wide

12 oz. white rolled fondant

blue, black, green, pink, yellow, and red edible food colors

small rolling pin

tracing or waxed paper

craft knife

sugar glue

modeling tools

pink dust

fine paintbrush

pastry bag

black royal icing for the eyes

method

1 Following the techniques on pages 140 and 142, cover the cake with marzipan and white fondant and place on a 9-inch round cake board covered with white fondant. Fix a length of ribbon around the cake board, tie the wider ribbon around the base of the cake, and finish with a double bow.

2 Color the paste for the Santa star as follows: a walnut-sized piece in pale blue, a walnut-sized piece in black, a walnut-sized piece in green, a hazelnut-sized piece in pale pink, a pea-sized piece in yellow; a walnut-sized piece in white, and the remainder in red.

3 To make the Santa star, start with the base red star which will form the body. Roll out the paste to a thickness of ⅛ inch and use the template on page 157 to trace and cut out a star with the craft knife. You can either fix this directly onto the top of the cake or place on a board dusted heavily with confectioners' sugar and allow to dry before gluing all together and fixing in to position later. Roll out and build up the second layer, using the templates to trace and cut out the gloves, boots, belt, tree, hat trim, face, and beard in the colors shown. Fix into position with sugar glue. Finish with the top layer—moustache, nose, and pom-pom for the hat. Dust Santa's cheeks with pink dust and a paintbrush until they are big and rosy! Pipe 2 black eyes using royal icing.

delicious treats

delicious treats In this chapter I give a collection of cake recipes that are delicious to eat—just as they are—for a weekend treat. Alternatively they can be covered with marzipan and icing or chocolate, and hand decorated. Whether your preference is for a rich, dark chocolate velvet cake or a lighter summer lime and coconut flavor, there is a recipe for all occasions. Throughout the book I have given my own personal cake preferences for each design—but this is by no means exhaustive and you can change the flavors to suit your own party occasion.

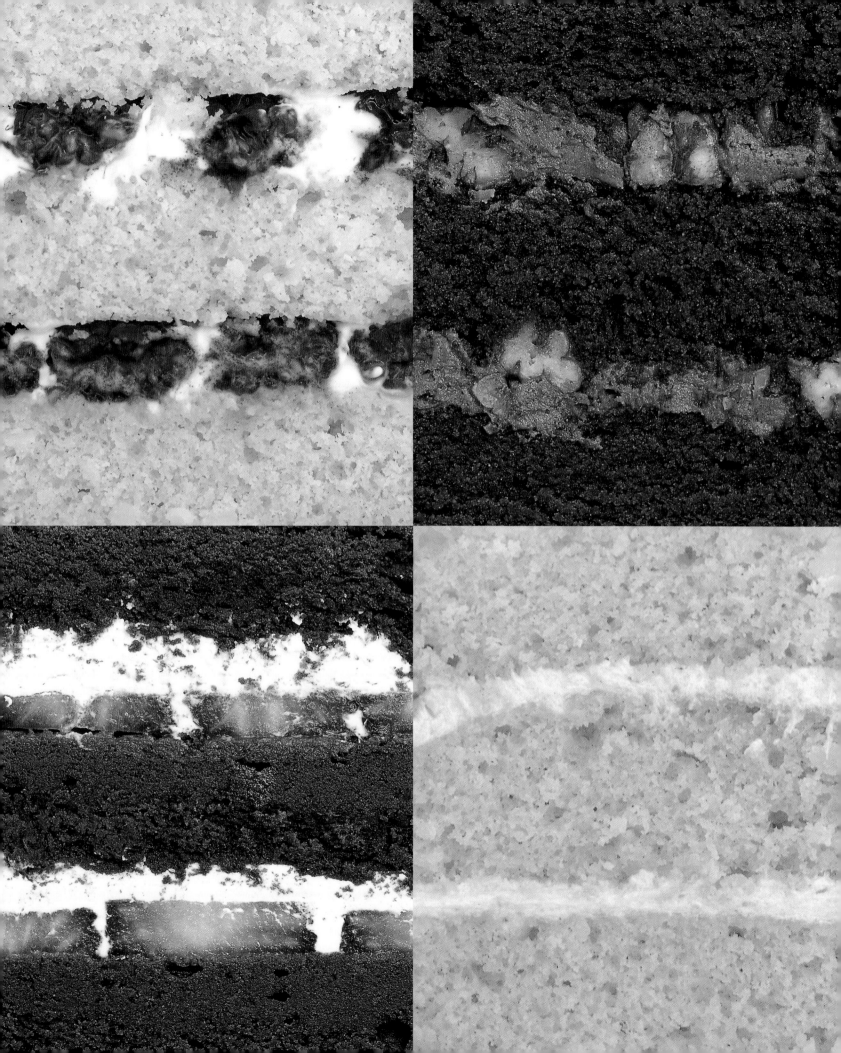

lime and coconut

This is a beautiful fresh cake combining the zest of fresh limes with creamed coconut. This cake is delicious to enjoy as it is, or use it as a base either for small or tiered party cakes, or individual cakes covered with icing and decoration as featured in earlier chapters.

for the cake

1 cup unsalted butter, softened

1 cup sugar

1¾ cups self-rising flour

4 free-range eggs, lightly beaten

2 tbsp milk

7 oz. block of creamed coconut

for the buttercream

zest and juice of 2 limes

⅓ cup unsalted butter, softened

scant 1 cup confectioners' sugar

⅔ cup toasted desiccated coconut to finish (or flakes)

method

1 Preheat oven to 375°F (convection oven 340°F). Grease two 8-inch springform pans and line the bottom with waxed or parchment paper. Grate the block of creamed coconut and keep half of it to one side.

2 Measure all the cake ingredients including half the creamed coconut into a large bowl and beat together until you have a smooth batter.

3 Divide the mixture into the two pans, smooth the surface and bake in the oven for 20–25 minutes until risen, light golden, and the cake springs back when pressed.

4 For the buttercream, mix together the reserved creamed coconut, zest and juice of 2 limes. Microwave or place over a pan of simmering water until the coconut melts. Allow to cool. Beat the butter until smooth and creamy, add the confectioners' sugar and beat slowly at first then at full speed until light and fluffy. Stir in the cooled coconut-lime mixture and beat until light and marshmallowy.

5 Sandwich the cakes with half of the buttercream and use the remainder on the top and sides of the cake. Sprinkle with the toasted coconut.

storage

Store in an airtight container and eat within 2 days. Not suitable for freezing.

tip

For individual cakes, bake 2 square halves then use each separately; split horizontally and fill with a thin layer of the buttercream.

vanilla with fresh raspberries

This vanilla cake is delicious served with fresh raspberries and mascarpone for a special treat. Other fresh berries can be substituted and the cake itself can be used for any of the covered and decorated designs featured in earlier chapters—especially the fondant cakes—if the filling is replaced with the Madagascan vanilla buttercream.

for the cake

1 cup unsalted butter, softened

1¼ cup granulated brown sugar

1 tbsp vanilla paste

4 large free-range eggs, lightly beaten

2 cups self-rising flour

3 tbsp milk

for the filling and decoration

2 tbsp confectioners' sugar

½ cup mascarpone

7 oz. fresh raspberries

alternative filling

¼ cup unsalted butter, softened

1 cup confectioners' sugar

2 tsp Madagascan vanilla extract

method

1 Preheat oven to 340°F (convection oven 300°F). Grease two 8-inch springform pans and line the bottom with waxed or parchment paper. Dust the sides with a little flour.

2 Using a hand mixer, cream together the butter and sugar until light and fluffy. Stir in the vanilla paste. Add the eggs a little at a time until well incorporated. If the mixture starts to separate and curdle, stir in 1 tbsp flour.

3 Fold in the remaining flour and stir in enough milk for a dropping consistency: the mixture should drop from the spoon by the count of three.

4 Spoon the mixture into the prepared pans. Level the top and bake in the oven for 25–30 minutes until well risen and a knife inserted in the center comes out clean. Allow to cool slightly before turning out onto a wire rack.

5 Fold the confectioners' sugar into the mascarpone then spread half over the bottom cake. Scatter half the raspberries on top. Place the other cake on top and repeat the mascarpone and raspberry layers. The cake can be kept up to 4 days ahead and stored in an airtight container. Refrigerate once filled with mascarpone and eat within 24 hours. Freezes for one month.

Madagascan vanilla buttercream

Cream the butter with an electric beater for 2 minutes until light and fluffy. Add the confectioners' sugar and beat slowly until incorporated, then on high speed until very light and fluffy. Beat in the vanilla extract. Keeps for one week in the fridge; allow to come up to room temperature before using and beat again.

banana butterscotch

The combination of smooth butterscotch and baked bananas makes this the perfect cake for afternoon tea on cold days. The butterscotch is poured into the cake as soon as it is baked, which keeps the cake lovely and moist, making it an ideal choice for further covering with marzipan, icing, and hand decoration.

for the cake

²/₃ cup unsalted butter
1¹/₃ cups self-rising flour
²/₃ cup granulated brown sugar
¹/₃ cup golden raisins
¹/₂ cup chopped walnuts
1 lb. bananas, mashed
2 free-range eggs
2 tsp vanilla extract

for the butterscotch

¹/₃ cup soft brown sugar
3 tbsp unsalted butter
2 tbsp heavy cream

method

1 Preheat oven to 350°F (convection oven 325°F). Grease a 8-inch round cake pan and line the bottom with waxed or parchment paper.

2 Rub the butter into the flour until the mixture resembles fine bread crumbs. Add the sugar, golden raisins, and chopped walnuts. Beat the bananas and eggs together until very thick and creamy, then fold in the dry ingredients and the vanilla extract.

3 Transfer to the prepared pan and bake in the oven for 1 hour 15 minutes until risen and firm to the touch.

4 About 10 minutes before the cake is due to come out of the oven, measure the butterscotch ingredients into a small saucepan and heat gently until the sugar has completely dissolved and is bubbling. As soon as the cake comes out of the oven, pierce it all over with a skewer and pour the bubbling butterscotch over the top. Leave to cool in the pan.

tip

For individual cakes, the cake will need to be split horizontally before cutting out the rounds or squares.

sticky date

When we baked the cakes in this chapter, this one was a clear favorite amongst the team. It is moist, sticky, and full of flavor. Because it requires no filling, this cake is an ideal choice for the base of the covered and decorated cakes in earlier chapters. It will stack well and keeps for a week once covered.

ingredients

1⅓ cups dates, pitted

1 cup unsalted butter, cut into pieces

2 cups dark muscovado sugar

2 free-range eggs

⅓ cup chopped preserved ginger in syrup

grated zest of 1 lemon

1 tsp vanilla extract

9 oz. granny smith apple, grated

1¾ cups self-rising flour

confectioners' sugar, for dusting

method

1 Preheat oven to 325°F (convection oven 275°F). Grease an 8-inch round kugelhopf cake pan.

2 Place the dates in a bowl and cover with boiling water. Melt the butter and sugar together in a saucepan and allow to cool slightly.

3 Beat the eggs, ginger, lemon zest, and vanilla extract into the butter and sugar. Drain the dates and chop finely. Add to the saucepan and mix well.

4 Stir in the apple and flour, then spoon into the pan and bake in the oven for about 1 hour 15 minutes until well risen. When done, a skewer inserted should come out clean with a few crumbs. Leave to cool in the pan.

5 Dust the top with confectioners' sugar to serve.

storage

The cake keeps a week stored in an airtight container or for 1 month frozen.

cherry and almond

This is a lovely moist cake as it combines fresh pitted cherries with a delicious crumble topping. Use the freshest, ripest cherries you can find. The finished cake is quite shallow which makes it the perfect depth for stamping out individual canapé-sized rounds to serve at a summer buffet party. It wouldn't require much accompaniment—maybe a nice spoonful of heavy cream. Because the cake contains fresh fruit, it is not suitable for covering with marzipan and icing and it needs to be eaten fresh or stored refrigerated.

for the cake

1 1/4 cups self-rising flour

1/4 cup granulated brown sugar

1 extra-large egg

4 tbsp organic milk

1/3 cup unsalted butter, melted

1 tsp almond extract

12 oz. juicy ripe cherries

confectioners' sugar, for dusting

for the crumble topping

2 tbsp butter at room temperature

1/4 cup ground almonds

5 tsp granulated brown sugar

1/2 tsp almond extract

method

1 Preheat oven to 350°F (convection oven 325°F). Grease and line the bottom of a shallow 8-inch cake pan. Measure the flour and sugar into a bowl and stir together. Make a well in the center and add the egg, milk, melted butter, and almond extract. Beat with an electric beater to make a smooth mixture. Spoon into the pan and spread evenly.

2 Remove the stems and pits from the cherries, cut in half, and scatter over the cake mixture. Gently press them in.

3 Make the topping by measuring all the ingredients into a clean bowl. Rub the butter in until the mixture resembles fine bread crumbs and then gently clumps together. Scatter over the cherries.

4 Bake for 30–35 minutes until a skewer inserted in the center of the cake comes out clean.

5 Allow the cake to cool before removing from the pan and allow to cool completely on a wire rack.

6 Dredge with confectioners' sugar to serve.

tip

Try substituting the fresh cherries with other ripe fruit in season—plums and apricots work particularly well—chop the pitted flesh into quarters before adding to the recipe.

chocolate and almond

This is a rich, indulgent chocolate cake baked without flour. The ground almonds provide a nutty taste and texture, and it holds together well and cuts beautifully. It is naturally shallow, which makes it a perfect cake for cutting out individual shapes to be used in the designs in earlier chapters of this book.

ingredients

½ cup unsalted butter, diced plus extra for greasing

flour, for dusting

5 oz. chocolate (70% cocoa solids), broken into pieces

6 large free-range eggs, separated

1⅓ cup ground almonds

1 tsp almond extract

⅓ cup superfine sugar

cocoa powder and whipped cream, to serve

method

1 Preheat oven to 340°F (convection oven 300°F). Grease a 9-inch springform pan and line the bottom with waxed or parchment paper. Dust the sides with a little flour.

2 Melt the unsalted butter and chocolate together in a bowl over a pan of simmering water—stir occasionally until smooth. Leave for 5 minutes to cool slightly.

3 Stir in the egg yolks, ground almonds, and almond extract.

4 Beat the egg whites in a separate clean bowl until soft peaks form. Continue beating, adding the sugar a spoonful at a time. Beat well between each addition until all is incorporated and stiff peaks form.

5 Stir 2 tbsp egg white into the chocolate mixture then gently fold in the remainder.

6 Spoon the mixture into the prepared pan and bake for 30–35 minutes until well risen and just firm to the touch. Dust with cocoa powder and serve with a spoonful of whipped cream.

storage

Can be kept up to 4 days ahead and stored in an airtight container. Freezes for one month.

espresso bites

These bites are ideal for entertaining guests with morning coffee or to serve as after-dinner treats. I have used the chocolate and almond cake (page 90) as the base, as this cake is naturally shallow and very "chocolaty." The espresso buttercream is flavored with real fresh espresso coffee and decorated with chocolate-covered espresso beans.

yields 25 bites

you will need

single layer 8-inch square cake, cut into 2 x 1½-inch slices

pastry bag

large star tip

cocoa

50 chocolate-covered espresso beans

espresso buttercream

espresso, made with 1¼ cup fresh espresso coffee and scant 1 cup fresh boiled water

1¼ cups unsalted butter, softened

3¼ cups confectioners' sugar, sifted

method

1 Cut the chocolate cake into 25 slices, each measuring 2 x 1½ inches.

2 Make the espresso buttercream. Make the coffee in a French press. Pour freshly boiled water onto the fresh ground coffee and allow to steep for 5 minutes. Strain the espresso and leave to cool slightly. Beat the unsalted butter until light and creamy. Add the confectioners' sugar and beat initially on slow then on high speed for 3 minutes. Stir in the espresso until you have the desired intensity of flavor.

3 Fill a pastry bag with a large star tip and the espresso buttercream. Pipe a swirl design of buttercream onto the top of each bite as shown. Sift a small amount of cocoa onto the top of each bite then finish with 2 chocolate-covered espresso beans on each cake.

3

tip

This technique works equally well with the lime and coconut cake with the lime and coconut buttercream, or the vanilla cake with vanilla buttercream. Serve a selection together for a large social gathering or party.

chocca mocca pecan

This cake has the perfect blend of smooth chocolate, fresh espresso, and toasted pecans. Delicious as a weekend cake to serve for family and friends, it can also be used as a base for any of the covered and decorated cakes throughout this book—especially the larger decorated celebration cakes and tiered options, whether covered with icing, fondant, or chocolate.

for the cake

5 oz. dark chocolate

4 tbsp strong brewed espresso

3/4 cup unsalted butter, softened

3/4 cup superfine sugar

5 large free-range eggs, lightly beaten

1 cup finely chopped pecans

scant 1 cup self-rising flour

1 tsp baking powder

for the filling and decoration

3 1/2 oz. dark chocolate

4 tbsp unsalted butter

3 tsp espresso coffee (use 3 rounded tablespoons of fresh coffee with scant 1 cup of freshly boiled water, then plunge in a French press)

4 tbsp heavy cream

1/3 cup confectioners' sugar

2/3 cup toasted pecans, roughly chopped

method

1 Preheat oven to 350°F (convection oven 325°F). Grease a 8-inch springform pan and line the bottom with waxed or parchment paper.

2 Melt the chocolate and espresso together over a pan of simmering water and stir until smooth. Allow to cool slightly.

3 Using a hand mixer, cream together the butter and sugar until light and fluffy. Beat in the eggs a little at a time until well incorporated. Don't worry if the mixture starts to separate and curdle, it won't affect the finished cake.

4 Pour in the chocolate mixture and add the pecans. Stir until combined.

5 Sift the flour and baking powder together in a separate bowl then gently fold into the cake mixture.

6 Spoon the mixture into the prepared pan and bake in the oven for 45–55 minutes until firm to the touch. Allow to cool slightly before turning out onto a wire rack to cool completely. Place the pecans for toasting on a baking tray and place in the oven for the final 10 minutes baking time. Remove and allow to cool before roughly chopping.

to make the filling

1 Put the chocolate, butter, espresso, and cream in a small pan and heat gently until dissolved and smooth. Remove from the heat and stir in the confectioners' sugar. Leave to cool then refrigerate for 1–2 hours until thick enough to spread.

2 Slice the cake horizontally and spread with half the filling. Scatter with half the toasted pecans. Cover with the other half of the cake, spread the remaining filling on the top, and finish with the remaining toasted pecans.

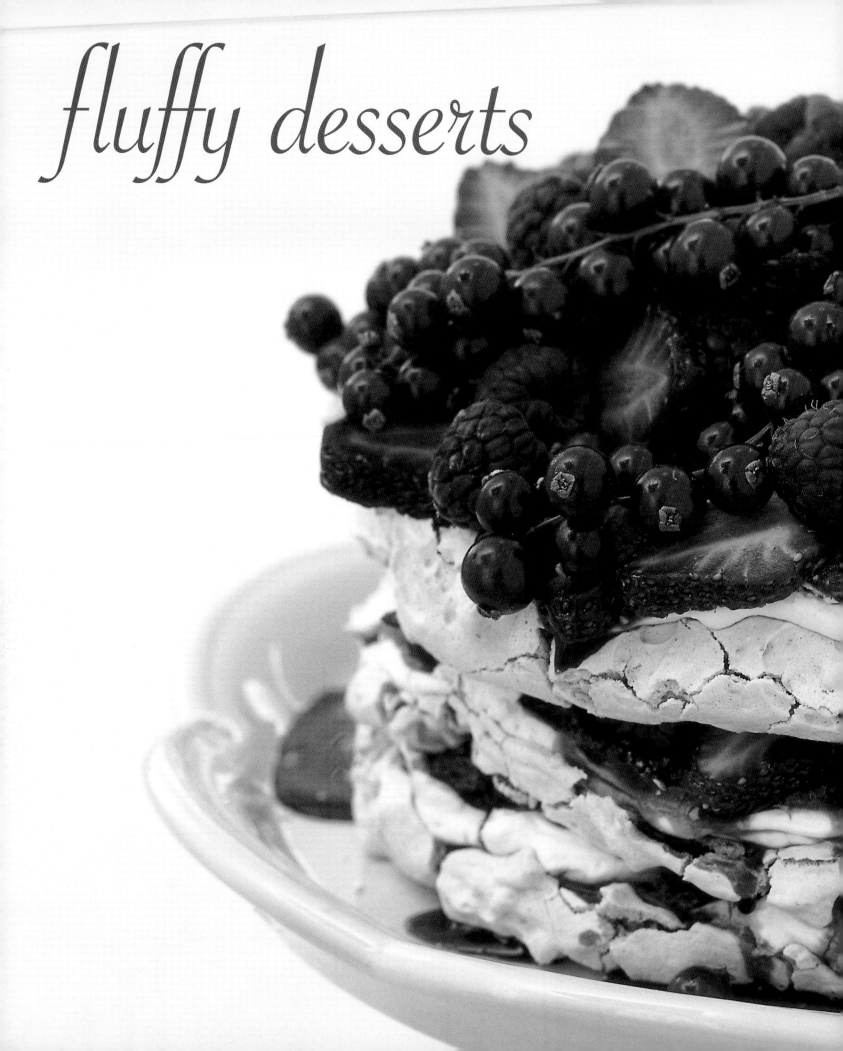

fluffy desserts

fluffy desserts I have had so much fun presenting— and tasting—this range of fabulous desserts and tortes. From creamy cheesecakes, to rich roulades, and mouthwatering meringues, these desserts make a fabulous addition to lunch or dinner parties and afternoon teas. Visually stunning and delicious to eat, they are guaranteed to impress and take only a fraction of the time of fully decorated cakes.

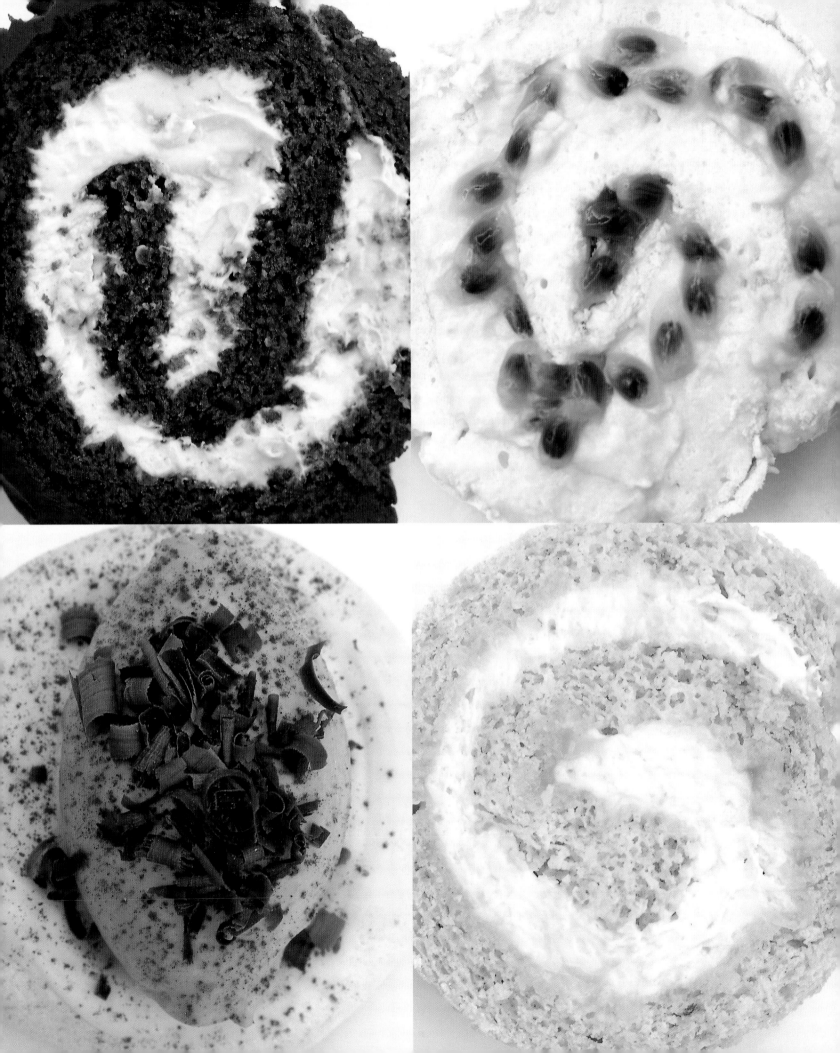

mango and ginger cheesecake

This recipe is one of my personal favorites and never fails to impress. It is simple to make as it needs no baking or setting agent: it relies on the weight of the cheese and cream to set the cheesecake. The combination of preserved ginger and fresh mango purée is absolutely delicious.

8–10 servings

fills eight 3-inch fluted tart pans or one 8-inch round

ingredients

1/3 cup unsalted butter

2 cups crushed graham crackers

12 oz. cream cheese

2/3 cup superfine sugar

2 drops vanilla extract

1 3/4 cups heavy cream

7 oz. fresh mango

2 pieces preserved ginger, chopped

2 tbsp preserved ginger syrup

method

1 Melt the butter in a saucepan and stir in the crushed graham crackers. Press into the base of a 8-inch springform tart pan and refrigerate for 1 hour or until set.

2 Beat the cream cheese, superfine sugar, and vanilla until light and fluffy. Add the cream and beat until stiff (but do not overbeat or the mixture will separate).

3 Process the fresh mango in the blender until it forms a thick purée. Stir 4 tbsp of the mango and the chopped preserved ginger into the cheesecake mix.

4 Spread the cheesecake mix on top of the cracker-crumb base and refrigerate overnight.

to serve

Stir the ginger syrup into the remaining mango purée and serve on the side.

chocolate cheesecake

A real adult's cheesecake and definitely one for chocoholics—for a more family-friendly version, omit the Kahlua. This cheesecake can be made a day in advance and the topping added just prior to serving.

for the base

4 tbsp unsalted butter

7 oz. dark chocolate-coated graham crackers, crushed

2 oz. amaretti cookies, crushed

for the filling

8 oz. dark chocolate (minimum 55% cocoa solids), broken

16 oz. full-fat cream cheese, at room temperature

1/2 cup superfine sugar

4 large eggs

1 1/4 cups heavy cream

5 tbsp Kahlua (optional)

for the topping

scant 1 cup heavy cream

2 tbsp Kahlua (optional)

cocoa powder, for dusting

2 oz. amaretti cookies, crushed

method

1 Melt the butter in a saucepan and stir in the crushed cookies. Press into the base of a nonstick 8-inch springform cake pan and refrigerate for 1 hour or until set.

2 Make the filling: melt the chocolate in a bowl over a pan of gently simmering water and allow to cool. Heat the oven to 325°F (convection oven 275°F).

3 Beat the cream cheese and superfine sugar until light and fluffy. Add the eggs one at a time but don't overbeat. Blend in the melted chocolate, the cream, and Kahlua (if using) slowly until combined then pour the cheesecake mix on top of the base. Bake in the oven for 1 hour until set.
Run a knife around the inside of the pan to loosen the cheesecake then refrigerate overnight.

to serve

1 Make the topping: combine the heavy cream with the Kahlua (if using). Lightly whip the cream and spread over the top of the cheesecake.

2 Mix the cocoa powder with the crushed amaretti cookies and sprinkle over the top.

black-currant cheesecake

This cheesecake has a traditional New York-style sour cream cheesecake base, which is deliciously creamy. I have added the sharpness of a black-currant compote as I grow the fruit in my garden and look forward to the juiciest crop for making this recipe every year. It makes a fabulous dinner party dessert and can be made a day in advance.

for the base

1/3 cup unsalted butter, plus extra for brushing the pan

1 1/3 cups crushed graham crackers

for the cheesecake filling

2 lb. full-fat cream cheese

1 1/4 cups superfine sugar

3 tbsp all-purpose flour

1 1/2 tsp vanilla extract

grated zest of 1 lemon

1 1/2 tsp lemon juice

3 extra-large eggs plus 1 yolk

1 1/4 cups sour cream

for the topping

2/3 cup sour cream

1 tbsp golden superfine sugar

2 tsp lemon juice

1 lb. 5 oz. black currants

1/3 cup granulated sugar

method

1 Heat the oven to 350°F (convection oven 325°F). Line the base of a 9-inch springform cake pan with waxed paper. Melt the butter in a saucepan and stir in the crushed crackers. Press into the base of the pan and bake for 10 minutes—allow to cool on a wire rack while preparing the filling.

2 Turn the oven up to 475°F (convection oven 400°F). In a large bowl, beat the cream cheese by itself until creamy, then slowly add the sugar and flour. Add the vanilla, lemon zest, and juice and beat for 2 minutes. Add the eggs and yolk one at a time. Stir the sour cream then add 1 cup to the cheesecake mixture (reserving the rest) and beat gently until smooth, light, and airy.

3 Place the pan on a baking sheet. Brush the sides of the pan with melted butter, then carefully pour in the cheesecake batter. Bake for 10 minutes then reduce the heat to 225°F (convection oven 195°F) and bake for an additional 25 minutes. Turn off the oven and open the door. Allow the cheesecake to cool for 2 hours; it may crack slightly on the top as it cools.

4 Make the topping: combine the reserved sour cream with the 2/3 cup sour cream, sugar, and lemon juice. Spread over the top of the cheesecake right to the edges. Cover loosely with foil and refrigerate for at least 8 hours or overnight.

5 Wash, top, and tail the black currants and place in a saucepan with the granulated sugar and a splash of water. Bring to the boil, then reduce the heat and simmer gently until the fruit has all broken up, 15–20 minutes. Remove from the heat and refrigerate overnight.

to serve

Run a round-bladed knife around the sides of the pan to loosen any stuck edges. Transfer the cheesecake onto a plate, and spoon the black currants on the top.

chocolate-strawberry torte

Chocolate and strawberries have such an affinity! This is an impressive recipe to serve for dessert; it encompasses layers of chocolate truffle torte sandwiched with fresh cream and succulent strawberries. The cake is smothered with a layer of chocolate buttercream before being covered with a deliciously wicked, thick chocolate glaze.

serves 12

for the cake

7 oz. plain chocolate (70% cocoa solids), broken into pieces

1¼ cups unsalted butter

2 cups light brown sugar

5 large eggs, beaten

1½ tsp vanilla extract

1¼ cups all-purpose flour, sifted

for the filling

7 oz. fresh strawberries

1¼ cups heavy cream

to finish

1 recipe chocolate ganache buttercream (see page 139)

1 lb. 2 oz. dark chocolate (70% cocoa solids), broken into pieces

generous 1 cup unsalted butter, cut into small pieces

generous ½ cup heavy cream

3½ oz. dark chocolate shards

method

1 Preheat the oven to 325°F (convection oven 275°F). Melt the chocolate carefully in a microwave or bowl over simmering water, then allow to cool. Have all the ingredients at room temperature. Grease and line a 8-inch cake pan. Beat together the butter and sugar until light and fluffy. Add the beaten eggs a little at a time until all are incorporated.

2 Pour the cooled melted chocolate slowly into the creamed mixture, beating all the time. Stir in the vanilla extract, then fold in the flour.

3 Pour the mixture in the pan and bake for 1 hour until risen and lightly set. The cake should still wobble when shaken lightly. Remove the cake from the oven and allow to cool before turning onto a wire rack. The crust should crack and sink back onto the cake.

4 To fill, carefully split the cake in half horizontally. Slice the fresh strawberries over the base. Lightly whip the cream and spread on top of the strawberries. Place the other cake layer on top. Stand the cake on a wire rack over a piece of waxed or parchment paper.

5 Make the chocolate ganache buttercream (see page 139). Using a palette knife, spread the buttercream over the top and sides of the cake filling all the gaps and leaving clean sharp edges and sides. Refrigerate for 30 minutes to firm before glazing.

6 Make the chocolate glaze. Place the chocolate and butter in a bowl. In a pan, bring the cream to the boil and pour over the chocolate and butter. Stir with a wooden spoon until the chocolate and butter have melted and the glaze is smooth. While it is still warm, pour the glaze liberally over the prepared cake. Use a palette knife or the back of a metal spoon to spread the chocolate over the cake top and sides. Holding the rack with both hands gently tap it to allow the chocolate glaze to even itself and settle over the cake. Decorate with dark chocolate shards as shown in the techniques on page 147.

chocolate-orange roulade

Chocolate and orange go together so well that this is an instant winner. It can be made in advance and filled prior to serving. Keep the orange cream well chilled so the filled roulade holds its shape. This recipe is rich and indulgent and forms a perfect centerpiece.

for the roulade

½ cup self-rising flour

1 tsp baking powder

¼ cup cocoa powder

½ cup ground almonds

5 extra-large eggs

½ cup superfine sugar, plus extra for turning out the cake

zest of 2 oranges

for the filling

1 lb. 2 oz. mascarpone

⅓ cup confectioners' sugar

zest of 2 oranges and 2 tbsp juice

for the frosting

7 oz. dark chocolate, broken into pieces

¾ cup unsalted butter, softened

⅓ cup confectioners' sugar

method

1 Heat the oven to 375°F (convection oven 340°F). Butter a 17 x 11-inch jelly-roll pan and line the base and sides with waxed or parchment paper.

2 Sift the self-rising flour, baking powder, and cocoa into a bowl and mix in the ground almonds. Put the eggs and superfine sugar in a large mixing bowl and beat for 5–10 minutes using an electric hand beater until pale and thick. The mixture should have tripled in volume and leave a trail when the beaters are lifted out. Fold the dry ingredients and orange zest into the egg mixture using a large metal spoon.

3 Pour the mixture into the prepared pan, ensuring all the corners are filled and even. Bake for 12–15 minutes until firm to the touch. Meanwhile, soak a clean kitchen towel in cold water and wring out. Lay this on a clean work surface with a sheet of waxed or parchment paper on top. Sprinkle the parchment with superfine sugar.

4 Once baked, remove the sponge from the oven and allow to cool for 1 minute before turning out onto the sugared paper. Peel away the baking paper in strips and with the short side facing you, roll the sponge up with the paper keeping the cold, damp cloth on the outside. Set aside until completely cold.

5 To make the filling, beat the mascarpone and confectioners' sugar with the fresh orange zest and juice. Unroll the roulade, discard the paper, and spread the mascarpone mixture over the entire sponge. Roll up carefully as tight as possible and transfer to a serving plate.

6 To make the frosting, melt the chocolate in a heatproof bowl over a pan of simmering water. Allow to cool for 10 minutes. Beat the butter and confectioners' sugar together until pale and smooth. Pour in the chocolate and stir thoroughly to combine. Set aside for 20 minutes to firm up slightly before spreading the frosting over the roulade with a metal spatula.

to serve

The roulade can be made up to a day in advance. Take it out of the fridge at least 30 minutes before serving to allow the filling and icing to soften.

lemon and lime roulade

Roulades are deceptively easy to make and always look very impressive when served. This roulade combines the fresh zest of lemons and limes for a light, refreshing dessert—it can be made a day in advance and filled prior to serving.

for the roulade

2 tbsp butter, plus extra for greasing

1 cup all-purpose flour, plus extra for dusting

4 eggs

½ cup superfine sugar

zest of 2 lemons

zest of 2 limes

for the filling

scant 1 cup heavy cream

zest of 1 lemon

zest of 1 lime

6 tbsp lemon curd

to decorate

confectioners' sugar

fresh edible flowers

method

1 Heat the oven to 350°F (convection oven 325°F). Butter a 17 x 11-inch jelly-roll pan and line the base and sides with waxed or parchment paper. Dust lightly with flour and chill.

2 Melt the butter then set aside to cool. Place the eggs and sugar in a large mixing bowl and beat until the mixture forms a thick trail (5 minutes), then briefly beat in the lemon and lime zests. Sift the flour into the mixture and gently fold in with a metal spoon. Pour in the cooled melted butter and gently fold in until well mixed.

3 Scrape the mixture into the prepared pan and spread with a metal spatula until it forms an even layer approximately ½-inch thick. Bake in the oven for 6–8 minutes until just cooked.

4 Soak a clean kitchen towel in cold water and wring out. Lay this on a clean work surface with a sheet of waxed or parchment paper on top. Sprinkle the parchment with superfine sugar. Invert the roulade onto the paper. Carefully roll the roulade up and leave aside.

5 To make the filling, whip the cream and fold in the zests of lemon and lime. Unroll the roulade and discard the paper. Spread the lemon curd and then the cream over the roulade and roll up tightly.

to serve

Heavily dust the top with sifted confectioners' sugar and decorate with fresh edible flowers.

storage

The roulade can be made up to a day in advance.

tip

Alternatively serve the cake with fresh summer berries and lightly whipped cream.

mango and passion fruit pavlova roulade

Making a roulade from meringue can seem quite daunting, but it is much easier to handle than it may appear. The elasticity of the egg whites helps to roll the roulade and it has a lovely light, soft texture with a crisp outer crust.

for the roulade

3 extra-large egg whites

¾ cup superfine sugar

1 level tsp cornstarch

1 tsp malt vinegar

1 tsp vanilla extract

confectioners' sugar, for dusting

for the filling

9 oz. mascarpone

1 large ripe mango, peeled, pitted, and finely chopped

⅔ cup heavy cream

2 passion fruits, pulp only

to decorate

confectioners' sugar

method

1 Heat the oven to 275°F (convection oven 250°F). Line a 12 x 9-inch jelly-roll pan with waxed or parchment paper.

2 Beat the egg whites with an electric beater until doubled in volume. Slowly beat in the superfine sugar until thick and shiny. Mix the cornstarch, vinegar, and vanilla extract, then beat into the egg whites.

3 Spoon into the pan and level the surface carefully, avoiding knocking out too many air bubbles. Bake for 30 minutes until the meringue surface is just firm. Meanwhile make the filling: beat the mascarpone and stir in the finely chopped mango. Whip the heavy cream until thick, then fold into the mango mix. Halve the passion fruit, scoop out the flesh, and set aside.

4 Remove the meringue from the oven and cover with damp waxed paper for 10 minutes. Dust another sheet of waxed paper with confectioners' sugar. Discard the damp paper and turn the meringue out onto the sugar-dusted paper. Peel the paper away from the back of the meringue in strips.

5 Spread the meringue with the mango cream and drizzle over the passion fruit. Roll up the roulade from the short side using the paper to assist and carefully transfer to a serving plate.

to serve
Dust liberally with confectioners' sugar.

storage
The roulade can be made up to a day in advance.

vanilla pavlova with chocolate and marron

These individual meringue cases are filled with a deliciously nutty marron cream, decorated with gentle shards of dark chocolate. They are ideal for a winter dinner party or autumnal cocktail party. The meringue can be made up to a week in advance and filled with the cream just before serving.

makes up to 20 individual meringues

for the meringue

3 large egg whites

¾ cup superfine sugar

1 tsp cornstarch

½ tsp vanilla extract

½ tsp white wine vinegar

5 oz. white chocolate

for the filling

scant 2 cups heavy cream

2 small cans sweetened chestnut purée (crème de marron)

3½ oz. dark chocolate, grated

method

1 Heat the oven to 275°F (convection oven 250°F). Line 2 large baking sheets with waxed or parchment paper. In a large bowl, beat the egg whites until stiff. Gradually beat in the sugar 1 tbsp at a time until the mixture is very stiff and shiny. Sift in the cornstarch then, using a large metal spoon, fold in along with the vanilla extract and vinegar. Place large tablespoonfuls of meringue mixture on the parchment paper and gently flatten each one to 3-inch diameter and make a light indent in each one.

2 Bake in the oven for 35–40 minutes until the meringue mixture is hard. Cool on a wire rack.

3 Melt the white chocolate and use a pastry brush to line each meringue case with white chocolate. Allow to set.

4 For the filling, whip the cream then fold in the sweetened chestnut purée.

5 With two dessertspoons, shape a oval quenelle of the filling and drop into the center of each meringue; top with grated dark chocolate.

pistachio meringue gâteau

This impressive meringue gâteau combines three layers of soft, chewy, nutty meringue with seasonal berries and fresh cream. It cuts beautifully and is perfect for a dinner party at any time of the year.

for the meringue

1¼ cups shelled pistachios

5 extra-large egg whites

1½ cups superfine sugar

1 tsp malt vinegar

1 tsp vanilla extract

for the red fruit compote

9 oz. strawberries

9 oz. raspberries

2 tbsp water

⅓ cup superfine sugar

for the filling

2½ cups heavy cream

9 oz. strawberries

9 oz. raspberries

¾ cup red currants

method

1 Heat the oven to 375°F (convection oven 340°F.) Line three 8-inch sandwich pans with waxed or parchment paper (alternatively draw three 8-inch circles on waxed paper, and place the paper on baking sheets).

2 Place the pistachios on a baking sheet and bake in the center of the oven for 10–15 minutes until golden brown. Allow to cool, then chop finely.

3 Place the egg whites in a clean, grease-free bowl and beat until stiff but not dry. Add the sugar gradually, beating well after each addition. When the mixture is very stiff, add the vinegar and vanilla extract.

4 Fold in the chopped nuts using a metal spoon. Divide the mixture between the 3 pans (or paper circles) and level the tops with the back of the metal spoon—dragging the top of one meringue into interesting peaks. Bake in the oven for 30–35 minutes until firm to the touch.

5 Leave in the pans to cool completely then turn out onto a wire rack and remove the paper.

6 To make the red fruit compote, put the strawberries, raspberries, water, and sugar in a pan. Bring to the boil then simmer for 20–25 minutes until reduced and the fruit has broken down. Allow to cool completely.

7 To fill the meringue gateau, whip the cream. Place the base meringue on a serving plate and spread over one third of the cream, drizzle 3 tbsp of the red fruit compote on top and one third of the fresh strawberries and raspberries; repeat with the second layer and finish with the third layer of meringue forming nice peaks. Spread with cream and fresh berries including the red currants. Serve the remaining red fruit compote in a separate dish on the side.

storage

The meringue can be made up to two weeks in advance and filled the day of serving.

cookies and pastries

cookies and pastries

Cookies and pastries are a fantastic addition to most parties. Themed, hand-decorated cookies can be served and eaten on the day, or packaged in clear cellophane or organza bags and presented as gifts or place settings. For more elaborate table-center decorations, I have included a "gingerbread house" using a traditional *Lebkuchen* recipe and the deliciously sweet traditional Persian sweetmeat baklava.

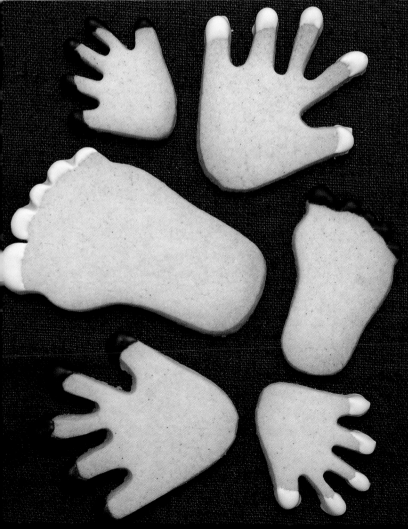

strawberry shortcake

The epitome of an English summer—conjuring up images of Wimbledon and cricket matches—these strawberry shortcakes are canapé-sized bites, making them perfect for summer buffet parties. Serve on a delicate cake stand accompanied by pink champagne, or place three *fraises des bois* in a glass and top up with sparkling wine.

makes 32

for the shortcake

¾ cup unsalted butter, softened

½ cup superfine sugar

zest of 1 lemon

1 tsp vanilla extract

1¼ cups ground almonds

1½ cups all-purpose flour, plus extra for dusting

for the filling

1¼ cups heavy cream

¾ cup little scarlet strawberry preserves

pastry bag and fluted tip

14 oz. *fraises des bois* or sliced strawberries

confectioners' sugar, for dusting

method

1 Cream together the butter and sugar until light and fluffy. Stir in the lemon zest and vanilla extract. Add the ground almonds and flour, and mix well to form a dough. Wrap the dough in plastic wrap and chill for 30 minutes. Preheat the oven to 325°F (convection oven 275°F). Line 2 baking sheets with waxed or parchment paper.

2 On a lightly floured surface, roll the dough to a thickness of ¼ inch. Cut out 2-inch rounds with a fluted pastry cutter. Lift onto the baking sheets with a metal spatula. Bake in the oven for 12–15 minutes until lightly golden. Leave to cool for 2 minutes then transfer to a wire rack until cold.

3 For the filling, whip the cream until firm.

4 Place a teaspoon of the preserves on the base of half the shortcake rounds. Using a fluted tip, pipe swirls of cream on top and add a slice of fresh strawberry or 3 *fraises des bois*. Place a disc of shortcake on top at a slight angle and dust with confectioners' sugar. Repeat with the remaining rounds.

flamingo cookies

Decorated cookies are a fabulous way to involve children with the cooking as the method is simple and the results instant. Here I have used flamingo cutters, but feel free to adapt for your own favorite cutter. For a more elaborate cookie that can be wrapped in a cellophane bag or boxed as a table setting or present, I have made flamingo cookies and decorated them with colored royal icing.

makes 12 large cookies

for the cookies

1 cup unsalted butter, softened

1 cup granulated brown sugar

1 large free-range egg, beaten

2 tsp pure vanilla-bean paste

3¹/₂ cups all-purpose flour, plus extra for dusting

shaped cookie cutter or template cut out of card

to decorate

1 recipe royal icing (page 145)

pastry bags

no. 1.5 tips

black, pink, and yellow edible food colors

paintbrush

clear cellophane bags

ribbon

method

1 Preheat oven to 350°F (convection oven 325°F). Gently cream the butter and sugar together then add the beaten egg to combine. Stir in the vanilla-bean paste. Gently fold in the flour and mix until the dough combines. Wrap the dough in plastic wrap and chill for 30 minutes.

2 Lightly flour a work surface and roll the dough out to a thickness of ¹/₄ inch. Stamp flamingo shapes out from the cookie dough and place well apart on a nonstick baking sheet.

3 Bake the cookies for 10 minutes until pale golden. Allow to cool slightly before transferring to a wire rack.

4 Fill a pastry bag with a no. 1.5 tip and white royal icing. Pipe the outline of the flamingo. Remove 1 tbsp icing, color black and transfer into a pastry bag with no. 1.5 tip.

5 Thin the remainder of the icing with water to a flooding consistency. Color three quarters pink, and one quarter yellow. Flood the pink body of the flamingo first using a paintbrush to reach all the corners and swirl a feather effect across the body. Allow to skin over before flooding the yellow legs and beak and finally piping the black legs, eye, and tip of the beak.

6 Allow to set overnight before wrapping in cellophane bags and tying with a pretty ribbon.

hands and feet cookies

Children love to be involved in baking these—as they are quick and easy to make—not to mention fun and delicious as well! For a simple finish, I have made vanilla and chocolate hands and feet and dipped the toes and fingers in melted chocolate.

makes 48 cookies

for the vanilla cookies

1 cup unsalted butter, softened

1 cup superfine sugar

1 large free-range egg, beaten

3½ cups all-purpose flour, plus extra for dusting

2 tsp pure vanilla-bean paste

for the chocolate cookies

replace ½ cup flour with ½ cup cocoa and omit the vanilla

to decorate

2½ oz. each white and dark chocolate, melted separately, for dipping the toes/fingers

method

1 Preheat oven to 350°F (convection oven 325°F). Gently cream the butter and sugar together then add the beaten egg to combine. Gently fold in the flour and vanilla paste and mix until the dough combines. Wrap the dough in plastic wrap and chill for 30 minutes.

2 Lightly flour a work surface and roll the dough out to a thickness of ¼ inch. Use cutters or templates to cut out the hands and feet and place well apart on nonstick baking sheets.

3 Bake the cookies for 10 minutes until pale golden.

4 Allow to cool slightly before transferring to a wire rack. When cold, dip the toes and fingers in the melted chocolate and leave to set on waxed paper.

tip

You needn't purchase expensive cookie cutters—trace a design onto cards and cut out around each one for a variety of designs. Vary the designs to suit the occasion. Decorated teapot shapes can look lovely served with afternoon tea.

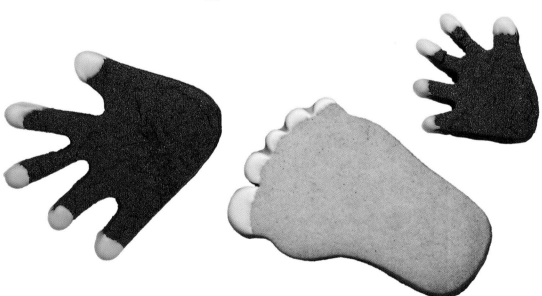

lebkuchen

One of the highlights of my year is visiting my sister in Munich for the annual Christmas markets in December. I can be guaranteed a biting wind, sufficiently potent Gluhwein, and warm, freshly baked, spiced *Lebkuchen*. Christmas has begun!

makes 40 individual cookies or 1 gingerbread house

for the Lebkuchen

½ cup unsalted butter, softened

¾ cup light muscovado sugar

1 large egg, beaten

⅓ cup molasses

3½ cups self-rising flour, plus extra for dusting

1 tsp ground ginger

½ tsp ground cloves

½ tsp ground chili

for covering and decorating

4 oz. milk chocolate, melted

4 oz. dark chocolate, melted

4 oz. white chocolate, melted

pastry bags

cocoa powder, for dusting

method

1 Cream together the butter and sugar until pale and fluffy. Beat in the egg and molasses. Sift the flour, ginger, cloves, and chili into the bowl. Use a wooden spoon to draw all the ingredients together until well mixed and it forms a stiff paste. Knead gently on a lightly floured work surface then wrap in plastic wrap and chill for 30 minutes. Preheat the oven to 350°F (convection oven 325°F). Line 2 baking sheets with parchment paper.

2 On a lightly floured surface, roll out half the dough to a thickness of ¼ inch. Cut out 2-inch heart shapes with a pastry cutter. Lift onto the baking sheets with a metal spatula. Divide the remaining dough into 20 pieces, roll into balls then place on the baking sheet. Flatten slightly with your fingers. Chill for a further 30 minutes.

3 Bake in the oven for 8–10 minutes. Transfer to a wire rack and allow to cool.

4 Melt and temper the chocolates (see page 147) separately in heatproof bowls over simmering water. Fill three small pastry bags with 1 tbsp of each of the melted chocolates.

5 With the cookies on a wire rack and a piece of waxed or parchment paper underneath the rack, use a metal spoon to cover each cookie with melted chocolate. Tap the rack gently to smooth and remove excess chocolate. Repeat with the three different chocolates until all cookies are covered. (If the chocolate starts to set, return the bowl over the heat.)

6 Dust several of the cookies with cocoa powder. Snip the end off the pastry bags while the chocolate is still warm and drizzle across the remaining cookies in a zig-zag design. Allow to cool and set before serving.

gingerbread house

The *Lebkuchen* recipe can be used to make individual cookies, covered in chocolate, or built into the most delightful gingerbread house— much easier than it looks and actually quite a lot of fun!

you will need

1 recipe Lebkuchen dough (page 127)

pastry bags

2 recipes royal icing (page 145)

no. 1.5, 2, 3, and star tips

edible glitter

10-inch round cake board

red and green edible food colors

jelly bean candies

2 oz. white rolled fondant

flower plunger-cutters

3½ oz. green rolled fondant

1 yard green ribbon ⅝-inch wide

method

1 Following the recipe on page 127, roll out the dough to a large square sheet to a thickness of ¼ inch, and bake in the oven at the given temperature.

2 Allow to cool slightly then cut out the base, 2 sides, 2 ends, 2 roof panels, and 2 pieces for the chimney with a large serrated knife, using the templates on pages 154–5.

3 Allow to cool completely. Fill a pastry bag with white royal icing and snip the end. Pipe a thick line of icing along the base edge of one side panel and attach to the base. Repeat with the other side. Next take the end panels and pipe a thick line of icing as shown and attach to the base and sides. Pipe a thick line of icing along the top edge of the 2 side panels and fix the roof into position with a thick line of icing along the join at the top. Stick the 2 chimney pieces together with a little royal icing. Allow to set.

4 Using a pastry bag filled with a star tip and white royal icing, pipe rows of stars along the center line of the roof and down both sides to cover the roof. Place the chimney pieces in position and cover the top with white royal icing. Sprinkle the icing with edible glitter. Allow to set.

5 Coat a cake board with white icing and use a metal spatula to texture a snow effect. Position the gingerbread house in the center of the board and decorate. Use colored icing to create windows and doors, and surround with jelly bean candies. Plunge flowers from the white fondant and fix these into position around the house. To make the trees, mold the green fondant into 3 cone shapes of different sizes. Snip around the cone with the end of a pair of small sharp scissors. Finish by fixing green ribbon around the base board.

storage

Keeps for 1 month.

nantucket ginger cookies

These hand-decorated ginger-spiced cookies look very festive, tied with ribbon on the Christmas tree, served on a pretty plate, or presented in cellophane bags or smart ribboned boxes.

makes 24 cookies

for the cookies

1/2 cup unsalted butter, softened

3/4 cup soft light brown sugar

1 tsp vanilla extract

1 1/2 cups all-purpose flour, plus extra for dusting

2 tbsp cocoa powder

2 tsp ground ginger

2 tbsp milk

for cutting, covering, and decorating

3-inch heart and star cookie cutters

large drinking straw

1 recipe royal icing, for piping (page 145)

red edible food color

pastry bags

no. 1.5 tips

1 recipe each white and red royal icing, for flooding (page 145)

gingham ribbon, 20 inches for each cookie including bow

method

1 Preheat the oven to 375°F (convection oven 340°F). Line a baking sheet with parchment paper. Cream together the butter, sugar, and vanilla extract until pale and fluffy. Sift together the flour, cocoa, and ginger. Work this in slowly to the creamed mixture adding a little milk to bind together.

2 Tip the dough onto a lightly floured surface and knead gently. Wrap the dough in plastic wrap and chill for 30 minutes.

3 Roll out the dough to ¼-inch thick. Stamp out heart and star shapes using a 3-inch cutter. Transfer to the baking sheet. Use the end of a large drinking straw to make a hole in the top of each cookie. Bake in the oven for 12–15 minutes until lightly golden. Leave on the baking sheets to cool, then remove to a wire rack to cool completely.

4 Divide the royal icing into two bowls and color one half with red edible color. Fill a pastry bag with a no. 1.5 tip and white royal icing. Pipe the outline on half of the hearts and stars. Fill a second pastry bag with white flooding icing and flood inside the lines. Repeat with the red icing on the other half of the cookies. Allow to set for 2 hours until a skin has formed on the cookies.

5 Fill a pastry bag with a no. 1.5 tip and red royal icing. Pipe a design in the center of all the white cookies—freehand but using the templates on page 156 as a guide. Repeat with white royal icing on the red cookies. Allow to set overnight.

6 Make a bow from the gingham ribbon for each cookie. Tie a length of gingham ribbon through the hole, fix the ribbon into position with royal icing and hang from the tree or serve on a pretty plate.

baklava

This is a traditional Persian sweetmeat served to celebrate the first official day of spring—March 21. The layers of thin pastry are interspersed with toasted pistachios and drenched in a delicious sweet syrup infused with rose water. Baklava is perfect served after dinner with coffee or fresh mint tea.

for the pastry

2½ cups finely chopped toasted pistachios

1 cup confectioners' sugar

⅔ cup unsalted butter, melted

1 lb. phyllo pastry

for the syrup

1½ cups granulated sugar

scant 1 cup water

2 tbsp rose water

method

1 Make the syrup. Place the sugar and water for the syrup in a saucepan, bring to the boil then reduce the heat and simmer for 10 minutes, until thickened. Stir in the rose water and set aside.

2 Mix together the nuts and confectioners' sugar. Preheat the oven to 325°F (convection oven 275°F). Brush a baking pan 7 x 11 x 2 inches with butter and line the base with waxed or parchment paper.

3 Taking one sheet of phyllo pastry at a time, and keeping the remainder covered with a damp cloth, brush with melted butter and lay in the baking pan. Repeat with 5 layers of pastry. Spread half the nut mixture over and press down with the back of a spoon.

4 Add another 5 layers of pastry, brush with butter and spoon over the remaining nuts. Finish with 5 layers of pastry. Cut the baklava into strips then diamonds and pour the remaining butter over the top. Bake in the oven for 20 minutes, then increase the temperature to 400°F (convection oven 350°F) and bake for additional 15 minutes until rich golden in color and well risen.

5 Remove from the oven and drizzle the syrup over the baklava. Allow to cool in the pan, then remove, gently tease the baklava apart with a sharp knife, and serve.

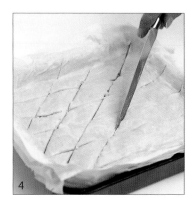

techniques

techniques In this section you will find the techniques needed to cover, ice, decorate, and stack my Party Cakes. I have included instructions for making royal icing, flooding icing, and fondant, as well as how to color rolled fondant and make sugar decorations. I show you how to temper chocolate before using it to create chocolate decorations, scrolls, and fans. Refer to these pages for the cakes in this book or use them for inspiration when creating your own designs.

buttercream

Buttercream is a combination of softened unsalted butter and confectioners' sugar. The basic mixture can be combined with other flavors: these orange, lemon curd, espresso and chocolate ganache versions are particularly good. For lime and coconut see page 80.

yields 1 lb. 11 oz.
ingredients
9 oz. unsalted butter, softened
1 lb. 2 oz. confectioners' sugar
1 tsp vanilla extract

Beat the softened butter for 2 minutes using an electric mixer. Sift in the confectioners' sugar and beat slowly at first. Add the vanilla extract then, with the mixer on full speed, whip until the buttercream is very light and fluffy.

fresh orange buttercream

Stir the grated zest of 2 fresh oranges and 4 tbsp juice into 1 recipe of buttercream. This buttercream works equally well layered between a vanilla cake or chocolate-based cake.

lemon curd buttercream

This buttercream is ideal as an alternative to fresh cream or mascarpone for filling the Vanilla cake (page 83) as it is shelf stable and suitable for use where the cake is to be covered in chocolate or marzipan and icing. Simply stir 10 oz. of lemon curd into 1 recipe of buttercream.

espresso buttercream

I particularly like this espresso buttercream as it is very indulgent. Use to top the Chocolate and Almond cake (page 90) or sandwich in the Chocca Mocca Pecan cake (page 95). Pour scant 1 cup freshly boiled water onto generous 1 cup of fresh ground coffee and allow to steep for 5 minutes. Strain the espresso and leave to cool slightly. Stir into 1 recipe of buttercream mixture until you have the desired intensity of flavor.

chocolate ganache buttercream

Chocolate ganache is a blend of boiled cream and chocolate. It has a smooth, rich, velvety texture that literally melts in the mouth. Mixed with buttercream, it becomes a wonderfully decadent filling or frosting.

ingredients

6 oz. dark chocolate (70% cocoa solids), broken into pieces

4½ oz. fresh heavy cream

1 recipe of buttercream

Place the chocolate pieces in a clean dry bowl. Bring the cream to the boil, remove from the heat, and pour over the chocolate. Stir with a wooden spoon until the chocolate is melted and the ganache is smooth and glossy. Allow the chocolate ganache to cool for 15 minutes before beating it into the buttercream. Store any excess buttercream in the refrigerator for up to 2 weeks.

cutting out small cakes

Individual cakes are stamped or cut out of a single larger tier. There will be wastage when cutting out round cakes—save this to create truffles or as the basis for a delicious trifle. An 8-inch square single layer cake will yield 16 2-inch individual cakes or 25 1½-inch canapé cakes. If using buttercream, split the layer of cake horizontally and spread with buttercream. Replace the top and use a round cutter to stamp out the cakes.

Cut rounds of cake using a 1½-inch cutter.

Cut an 8-inch square cake into 20 slices, each measuring 2 x 1½ inches. Use a ruler as a guide or cut a 2-inch template in thick card.

marzipan

One question I am often asked is: "Do I have to use marzipan?" Some seem to love, and some loathe, this luxurious almond paste. In fact, marzipan plays a threefold role as a covering for a cake: firstly, it protects the cake, locking in moisture; secondly, it adds form and stability—especially if the cake is for a tiered cake; thirdly, it provides a good clean base for the icing, which prevents the color of the cake bleeding through. For multi-tiered cakes I recommend it as essential; however, you could cover a single-tier cake with a double layer of rolled fondant instead if you wish.

covering a large cake with marzipan

you will need

cake

thin board the same size as the cake

pastry brush

boiled, sieved apricot jam

marzipan

confectioners' sugar

rolling pin

smoother

turntable or bowl

sharp knife

1 Place the cooled, baked cake upside down on a thin cake board the same size as the cake and brush liberally with boiled, sieved apricot jam. Knead the marzipan until smooth and pliable. Dust the work surface lightly with confectioners' sugar and roll the marzipan evenly into a size large enough to cover the top and sides of the cake, allowing for surplus (use string to measure). The marzipan should be approximately ¼-inch thick. Carefully lift the marzipan onto the cake.

2 Smooth the top and sides of the cake using your hands and a smoother. Trim off the majority of the excess marzipan.

3 Lift the cake onto a turntable or upturned bowl and neatly trim the final excess marzipan using a sharp knife and keeping it flush with the bottom of the board.

TIP alternatively, for those who loathe marzipan, cover the cakes with an initial layer of white chocolate plastique prior to covering with rolled fondant.

1

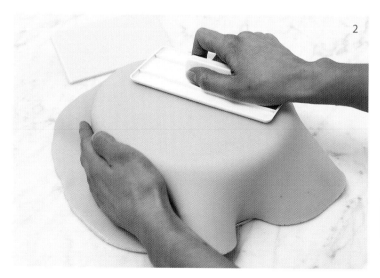

2

3

covering an individual round cake with marzipan

Individual cakes need to be perfectly covered with marzipan and rolled fondant before they are decorated. This is a skilled process, which requires practice and patience. All individual cakes are cut from one large cake: rounds are stamped out with a cutter and square cakes are cut with a sharp knife. Whether the cakes are square or round, covered with marzipan and fondant, or chocolate plastique, the techniques are very similar.

1 Brush the sides and top of the cakes with boiled, slightly cooled apricot jam.

2 Roll out the marzipan to a thickness of ⅛-inch and cut into squares approximately 6 x 6 inches. Place a square over each cake and press down all the way round.

3 Use a slightly larger cutter (2-inch for canapé size or 2½-inch for individual size), carefully position over the marzipanned cake and stamp out. Remove the excess marzipan. Use 2 straight edge smoothers together to flatten the top and neaten the sides and bottom edge.

gum paste and modeling paste

Ready-made gum paste or modeling paste is available from most cake decorating stores. It dries harder and can be rolled more thinly than fondant, allowing for larger models or finer flowers. It will keep for up to 1 month wrapped in plastic wrap, in an airtight container.

yields 1 lb.
2 tsp powdered gelatine
1 lb. confectioners' sugar, sifted
3 tsp gum tragacanth
2 tsp light corn syrup
2 tsp vegetable shortening
1 egg white

1 Soak the gelatine in 5 tsp cold water for 30 minutes. Meanwhile heat the confectioners' sugar and gum tragacanth in a bowl over a saucepan of hot water.

2 Dissolve the light corn syrup, vegetable shortening, and gelatine over a low heat.

3 Beat the sugar mixture in an electric mixer at low speed. Add the syrup mixture and egg white. Turn to maximum speed and beat for 15 minutes.

rolled fondant

Rolled fondant is a wonderful invention. Rolled out like marzipan and smoothed over the cake, this sweet paste creates a fast, clean, smooth finish with gently curved edges. It is soft and pliable to apply; sets firm but not rock hard; cuts beautifully; and has a shelf life of one year. However, it does not like to get wet—moisture will dissolve the sugar leaving craters, so keep all utensils clean and thoroughly dry.

covering a large cake with rolled fondant

1 Brush the thick baseboard with cooled boiled water. Dust the work surface lightly with confectioners' sugar (too much will dry the fondant) and knead the fondant until smooth and pliable. Evenly roll the fondant to the correct size—large enough to cover the baseboard and approximately ⅛-inch thick. Carefully place the fondant over the board and use a smoother to finish. Holding the board in one hand, use a sharp knife to cut away the excess, keeping the knife flush with the side of the board. Set aside to set (ideally overnight).

2 Brush the marzipan-covered cake with brandy or cooled boiled water. This acts as a good antiseptic seal between the marzipan and fondant as well as being an adhesive.

3 Dust the work surface lightly with confectioners' sugar and knead the fondant until smooth and pliable. Evenly roll the fondant into a size large enough to cover the top and sides of the cake, allowing for surplus (use string to measure). It should be approximately ¼-inch thick. Carefully lift the fondant onto the marzipan-covered cake.

4 Smooth the top and sides with your hands, carefully pressing the fondant against the cake. Be careful not to drag the fondant down the sides of the cake as this will cause it to crack and tear.

5 Use a smoother to give the cake a professional, clean finish and prick any air bubbles with a pin. Trim most of the excess fondant away from the cake.

6 Lift the cake onto a turntable or upturned bowl and neatly trim away all the excess fondant using a sharp knife, keeping the knife flush with the bottom of the board. Slide a metal spatula carefully underneath the cake and board and lift from underneath using both hands. Put a dab of royal icing on the prelined baseboard and carefully set the cake in position on top.

you will need

marzipan-covered cake placed on a thin board of the same size

pastry brush

thick board 3 inches larger than the cake

confectioners' sugar

rolled fondant

rolling pin

smoother

sharp knife

brandy or cooled boiled water

turntable or bowl

metal spatula

small quantity of royal icing

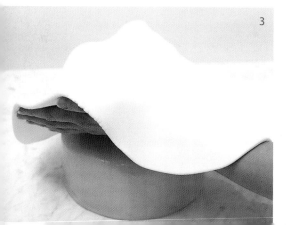

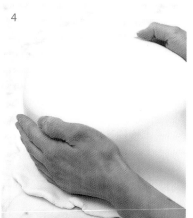

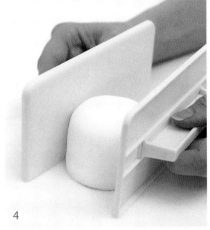

1 2

3 4

covering an individual round cake with rolled fondant

Individual cakes are covered with a top coat of fondant once they have been covered either with a layer of marzipan or white chocolate plastique (for those who dislike marzipan) This will set firm overnight to allow handling and additional decoration.

1 Brush the marzipan-covered individual cake with brandy or cooled boiled water to help the fondant adhere.

2 Roll out the fondant to a thickness of ⅛ inch and cut into squares approximately 8 x 8 inches. Place a square over each cake and press down all the way round.

3 Use a slightly larger cutter (2½ inch for canapé size or 3 inch for individual size), carefully position over the iced cake and stamp out. Remove the excess fondant.

4 Use 2 straight edge smoothers together to flatten the top and neaten the sides and bottom edge.

coloring rolled fondant

Commercially colored fondant is available to purchase, which can be helpful for covering a number of individual cakes or a larger tiered cake. However, for smaller quantities or more control over the exact color it is simple to color your own.

1

2

3

1 Knead a ball of white fondant on a clean surface lightly dusted with confectioners' sugar. Edible colors specifically formulated for sugar craft are more concentrated and come as a paste. Insert a wooden pick or washable plastic doweling rod into the color paste. Drag it across the top of the fondant as shown.

2 Gently knead the fondant until the color is uniform throughout.

3 Test this by cutting the fondant cleanly through the center.

TIP try not to use too much confectioners' sugar as this will dry the fondant out. If the fondant begins to show signs of cracking, work a little vegetable shortening into it. Add enough edible coloring paste to create the desired intensity of color.

TIP for dark colors or if coloring a number of different fondants, wear disposable gloves to avoid coloring your hands.

fondant

Fondant powder is available commercially—composed of confectioners' sugar and glucose powder. Use 2 tsp water per 3½ oz. fondant powder and allow 2½ oz. icing per individual cake. Spoon it over each cake or invert each cake and dip into the fondant using a dipping fork.

covering a cake with fondant

1   Measure the fondant powder into a large bowl. Make a well in the center and measure in the cooled boiled water.

2   Mix the fondant with a wooden spoon to a paste. This is the point to color the fondant if desired.

3   Use a small amount of color on the end of a wooden pick. Blend with a wooden spoon.

4   Warm the fondant either over a pan of simmering water or for a brief time in a microwave. The fondant should be warmed to body temperature (98°F) so it is just warm to the touch. The fondant should be less viscous at this stage. Use a large spoon and place the cake on a wire rack over a sheet of nonstick baking parchment. Carefully pour the fondant over the cake, using the back of the spoon to encourage it down the sides until they are fully covered.

5   Carefully remove the covered cake with a metal spatula.

6   Position in a pretty paper case. Gather the sides around the cake and hold in position either with a length of tied ribbon or a rubber band until the icing has set firm.

5

6

royal icing

Royal icing is used for adding hand decoration to cakes, or thinned for flooding run-outs. Once made, royal icing will keep fresh in an airtight container for up to 7 days. It will separate if left for longer than 24 hours and should be rebeaten before using.

yields 14 oz.
ingredients
1 large egg white
2¼ cups confectioners' sugar, sifted
juice of ½ lemon, strained

Place the egg white in a clean, grease-free bowl and beat until it forms very soft peaks. Add the confectioners' sugar and beat slowly at first until all the sugar is incorporated, then on full speed for 1 minute. Add the lemon juice and beat for another minute.

flooding icing

Flooding icing is used to fill the royal-iced outlines for making run-outs. I have used this technique in several recipes including the decoration on the rolled fondant discs for Coconut Butterflies on page 27.

Thin the royal icing down with drops of egg white or water. Egg white will make the finished run-out stronger but the icing may take longer to dry. Thinning the icing with water will enable it to dry quicker but it will be less strong. Add additional liquid a drop at a time to the royal icing and stir gently. Do not beat the icing as you will incorporate too much air and bubbles will appear in the run-outs. To judge the amount of water to add, swirl a knife in the bowl and count steadily to 10 as the ripples subside.

ingredients
1 recipe royal icing
egg white or water
food coloring

using flooding icing to make a butterfly

This technique is used to decorate Sugar Candy (page 67).

1 Trace a selection of butterfly designs (see page 152) onto tracing paper and fix a piece of waxed paper over the top, shiny side up, holding both in position with masking tape. Using a no. 1.5 tip and white royal icing, pipe the outline.

2 Separate the flooding icing into 3 bowls, color one yellow and one green, leaving one white. Fill 3 pastry bags with the icing and flood the butterflies, making some with each color. Use a small damp paintbrush to pull the icing to fill all the corners.

3 While the icing is still wet, add detail with a contrast color inside the wings and drag with a wooden pick to form patterns. Allow to set for 15 minutes then flood the lower wings. Leave the iced butterfly wings overnight to dry.

4 Peel the butterfly wings from the waxed paper. Fill a pastry bag with a no. 3 tip and reserved royal icing. Pipe a head and body onto clean waxed paper and then attach wings onto the iced body at an angle, supporting each one with a small piece of sponge. Insert 2 stamens for antennae. Leave to dry overnight. When dry, attach the butterflies to the cake using a small amount of royal icing.

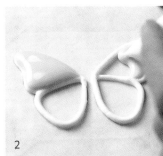

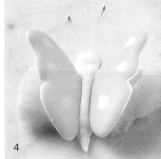

making a pastry bag

Pastry bags are made from triangles of waxed or parchment paper. The larger the triangle, the larger the pastry bag. I like to make various sizes—smaller ones for flooding lots of different colors and larger ones for piping single colors onto a number of tiers.

1 Fold a 12 to 18-inch square of waxed paper in half diagonally to make 2 triangles and cut the paper in half along the crease. Place the paper on the table with the tip of the triangle facing you and bring the underside of the left point to the right of center and hold with your thumb and forefinger.

2 Bring the right hand point up, over and round to the back to meet the center.

3 Carefully fold the corner of the paper over to secure the bag, as shown.

stacking tiers

Covered 2-inch cakes can be stacked directly onto a larger tier without the need for a baseboard or doweling rods. For all cakes 3 inches or larger being stacked, they should first be covered on a board the same size as the cake, and the bottom tier should be doweled to prevent the tiers collapsing or sinking.

1 Insert a doweling rod into the center of the bottom cake. Use a pencil to mark the point on the doweling rod which is level with the top of the cake. Remove the doweling rod. Line this doweling rod up with 4 others and mark them all level with the guide mark. Cut the doweling rods cleanly at the mark and check they are all the same length. Reinsert the central doweling rod and 4 others around the sides, spread out but keeping within the dimensions of the upper tier.

2 Smear a small amount of royal icing on the top of the bottom cake.

3 Carefully lift the top tier into position. Slide the cake carefully until it is positioned centrally or purposely offset.

chocolate

I like to cover individual cakes with pure melted chocolate. The taste and finish is a clean, crisp chocolate with all the appeal of a decadent chocolate truffle. In order to work effectively with melted chocolate, it must first be tempered (or pre-crystallized) to achieve the shine, correct melting properties, and stability required. Most importantly, tempering will prevent blooming (unsightly white streaks in the chocolate as it resets).

tempering chocolate

1 Break the chocolate into small pieces and place in a large clean bowl over a pan of simmering water. (Do not boil—if water or steam comes into contact with the chocolate, it will turn into a solid block. Water and chocolate do not mix!) Stir the chocolate while melting to ensure even heating but try to avoid creating air bubbles. Heat chocolate to 113°F.

2 Replace the hot water with cold water and stir continuously until the chocolate cools to 81°F. Occasionally it may be necessary to add additional cool water underneath the bowl.

3 Replace the cold water with warm water and raise the temperature of the chocolate to between 89°F and 90°F for

dark chocolate, 86°F and 89°F for milk chocolate, and 82°F and 84°F for white chocolate. Maintain the appropriate temperature while dipping. If the chocolate cools or warms outside of these temperatures, you will need to repeat the tempering process.

4 Test the temper of the chocolate before starting to dip. This can be done by spreading a small amount onto aluminum foil and allowing it to cool. It should be smooth and shiny with no dull or wet areas. Streaks may indicate poor temper or a lack of mixing. If the results are unsatisfactory, you will need to retemper the chocolate before proceeding.

making chocolate decorations

These are made from sheets of tempered chocolate and can be prepared in advance, then stored in an airtight container for up to 3 months. Use them to add the finishing decorations on any number of cakes, such as Marbled Chocolate Truffles (page 14).

1 **Chocolate scrolls** Spread the freshly tempered chocolate onto a clean marble slab or stainless steel baking tray to a thickness of 1/16 inch. Using a specialized chocolate scraper, carefully push the scraper along the right hand edge of the chocolate as it begins to set, making a strip about 3/4 inch wide and about 2 inches long, until the chocolate has curled around twice. For chocolate shards as used on the Chocolate-Strawberry Torte (page 106), allow the chocolate to set firm. Use this same technique to gather shards as the chocolate will be too hard to curl over itself.

2 **Chocolate fans** A similar technique to the scrolls—spread the tempered chocolate out as before. Once the chocolate begins to set, use the scraper along the right-hand side of the chocolate holding your finger along the edge of the scraper and chocolate as shown.

3 **Chocolate curls** Pour the freshly tempered chocolate into a small plastic container to a thickness of at least 1/2 inch. Allow to set completely. Holding the block of chocolate in one hand, carefully pull a vegetable peeler across the chocolate to create the curls.

chocolate plastique

Chocolate plastique is a combination of pure chocolate with a sugar stock syrup—effectively glucose—which makes chocolate malleable, enabling you to roll it out to cover a cake or hand mold it to create the fans, roses, and leaves used in many of the designs shown here. It has all the taste of chocolate, but with the texture of fondant and gives a smooth, firm finish to a cake. You can use chocolate plastique to cover a cake in exactly the same way as you would marzipan and rolled fondant. To make milk chocolate plastique, knead together dark and white chocolate plastique.

plastique stock syrup

yields 9 fl. oz.

ingredients

9 fl. oz. water

²⁄₃ cup superfine sugar

3 oz. light corn syrup

Place all the ingredients in a saucepan and bring to the boil. Remove from the heat and leave to cool. This recipe will provide slightly more than necessary to create the white chocolate plastique recipe below.

white chocolate plastique

yields 5 lb. 8 oz.

ingredients

3 lb. 14 oz. white chocolate, broken into pieces

4 oz. cocoa butter

14 oz. light corn syrup

10 fl. oz. stock syrup

1 Melt the chocolate in a microwave or place it in a clean, heat-resistant bowl over a saucepan of simmering water. Melt the cocoa butter in a microwave or place it in a clean, heat-resistant bowl over a saucepan of simmering water. (It is important to melt the cocoa butter and chocolate separately as they melt at different rates and both need to be melted for the recipe to work.) Mix the chocolate and cocoa butter together and stir well. Measure the light corn syrup and stock syrup together and warm slightly in the microwave. (This allows all the ingredients to be at a similar temperature for the final mix.)

2 Pour chocolate over light corn and stock syrups and mix well with a wooden spoon until smooth. Transfer the mixture into a clean large freezer bag and leave overnight at room temperature to set.

3 When ready to use, knead the chocolate plastique until smooth and pliable. Roll out on a work surface lightly dusted with confectioners' sugar.

dark chocolate plastique

This paste is quite firm and chewy. Use this recipe for making hand molded roses, lilies, and other decorations but mix it 1:1 with white rolled fondant for covering cakes.

Melt the chocolate in a microwave or place it in a clean, heat-resistant bowl over a pan of simmering water. Heat to 110°F. Heat the light corn syrup separately to the same temperature. Pour the syrup into the melted chocolate and stir with a wooden spoon until thoroughly combined. Allow to cool completely. Transfer the mixture into a clean, large freezer bag and leave overnight at room temperature to set. To use, peel away the bag and knead the chocolate until smooth and pliable.

yields 5 lb.

ingredients

1 lb. 12 oz. dark chocolate (55% maximum cocoa solids), broken into pieces

2 lb. 4 oz. light corn syrup

covering an individual square cake with chocolate plastique

Individual cakes can be covered with white chocolate plastique with a final coat of either rolled fondant, or white or dark chocolate plastique. Cut the cake into squares using a ruler and a sharp knife as shown on page 139. Cut the individual cakes into 2-inch squares, or canapé size 1½-inch squares. Brush the sides and top of the cakes with boiled, slightly cooled apricot jam.

1 Roll out the chocolate plastique to a thickness of ⅛ inch and cut into pieces approximately 6 x 6 inches square. Place a square over each cake and press down all the way round.

2 Square the sides using 2 straight-edge smoothers.

3 Trim the excess paste with a sharp knife. Use the smoothers again to flatten the top and neaten the sides and bottom edge. Repeat with the top coat, which can be dark or white chocolate plastique or rolled fondant.

1

2

3

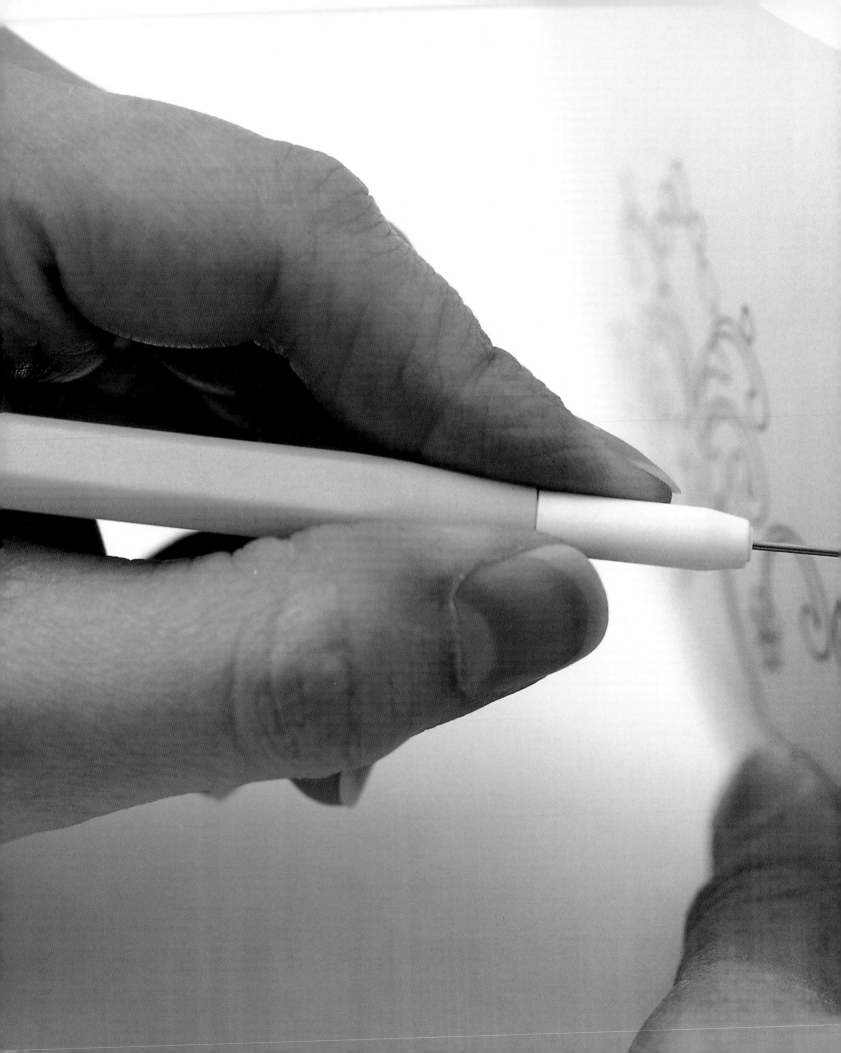

templates

bugs and butterflies

see page 28

bollywood

see page 22

coconut butterflies

see page 27

bunny alphabet block

see page 71

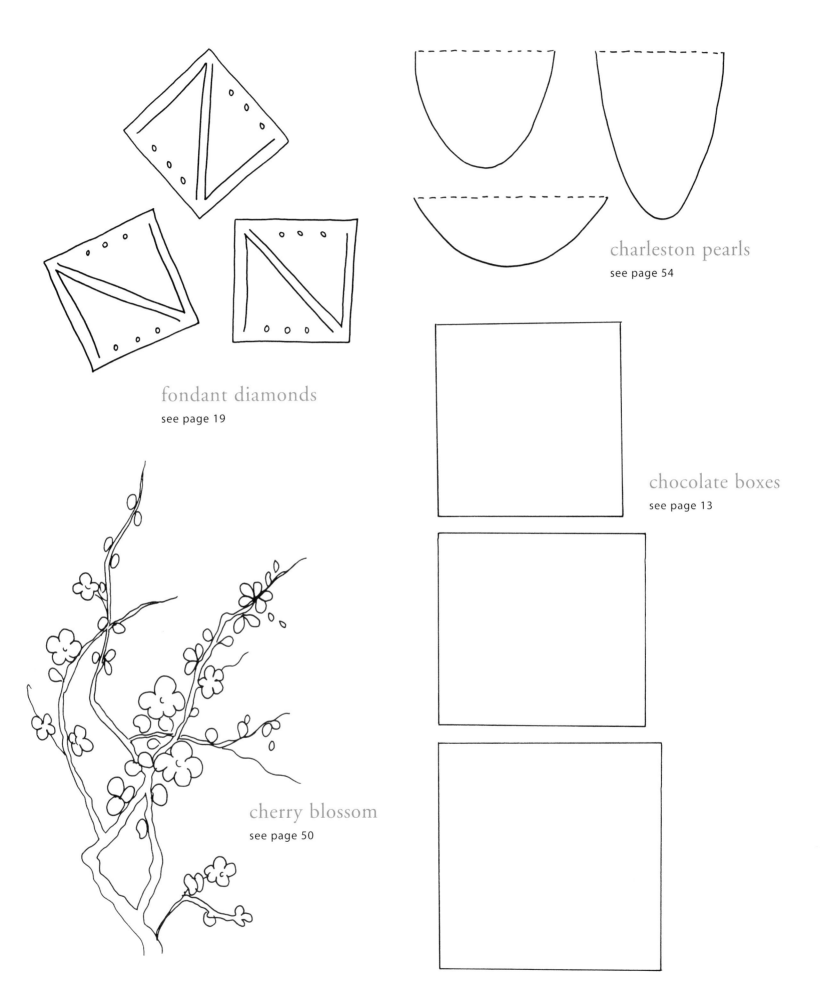

fondant diamonds

see page 19

charleston pearls

see page 54

chocolate boxes

see page 13

cherry blossom

see page 50

little venice lace™
see page 53

gingerbread house
roof panel (make 2)
see page 128

christmas canapé collection
see page 30

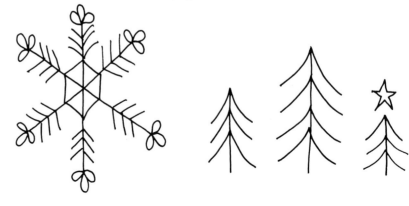

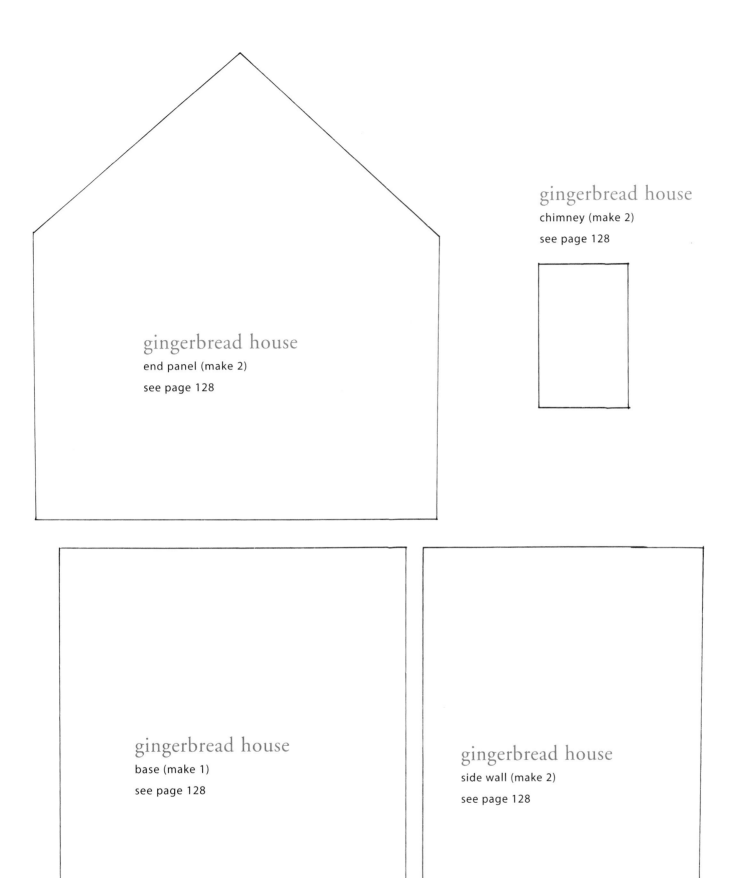

gingerbread house

end panel (make 2)

see page 128

gingerbread house

chimney (make 2)

see page 128

gingerbread house

base (make 1)

see page 128

gingerbread house

side wall (make 2)

see page 128

metallic painted irises

see page 58

monochrome lace

see page 20

nantucket ginger cookies

see page 130

santa star

see page 74

santa star

see page 74

santa star

see page 74

useful addresses

Beryl's Cake Decorating & Pastry Supplies
P.O. Box 1584
North Springfield, VA 22151
Phone: 1-800-488-2749 / 1-703-256-6951
Fax: 1-703-750-3779
www.beryls.com

Broadway Panhandler
65 East 8th Street
New York, NY 10003
Phone: 1-212-966-3434 / 1-866-COOKWARE (266-5927)
Fax: 1-212-966-9017
www.broadwaypanhandler.com

Kitchen Krafts
P.O. Box 442
Waukon, IA 52172-0442
Phone: 1-800-298-5389 / 1-563-535-8000
Fax: 1-800-850-3093 / 1-563-535-8001
www.kitchenkrafts.com

New York Cake & Baking
56 West 22nd Street
New York, NY 10010
Phone: 1-800-942-2539 / 1-212-675-2253
Fax: 1-212-675-7099
www.nycake.com

Pastry Chef Central, Inc.
1355 West Palmetto Park Road, Suite 302
Boca Raton, FL 33486-3303
Phone: 1-888-750-CHEF (2433) / 1-561-999-9483
Fax: 1-561-999-1282
www.pastrychef.com

Pattycakes, Inc.
34-55 Junction Boulevard
Jackson Heights, NY 11372-3828
Phone: 1-866-999-8400 / 1-718-651-5770
www.pattycakes.com

Sugarcraft
2715 Dixie Highway
Hamilton, OH 45015
Phone: 1-513-896-7089
www.sugarcraft.com

Sweet Celebrations, Inc.
(formerly Maid of Scandinavia)
P.O. Box 39426
Edina, MN 55439-0426
Phone: 1-800-328-6722 / 1-952-943-1508
www.sweetc.com

The Ultimate Baker
4917 East 2nd Street
Spokane Valley, WA 99212
Phone: 1-866-285-COOK (2665) / 1-509-954-5753
Fax: 1-225-410-9048
www.cooksdream.com

Wilton Industries
2240 West 75th Street
Woodridge, IL 60517
Phone: 1-800-794-5866 / 1-630-963-1818
Fax: 1-888-824-9520 / 1-630-963-7196
www.wilton.com

index

acknowledgments

Party Cakes for Fantastic Party People—many of whom I would like to thank for all their hard work, patience and support in the preparation of this book, and in the sampling this collection of mouthwatering cakes, puddings and sweet treats.

Thank you to my talented team at Little Venice Cake Company—especially Alison Thompson—another of my fine pastry chefs now back in Australia!—who so ably assisted with the Fluffy Desserts and chocolate work. Thank you to Christine Lee for your constant banter and intricate hand decorating skills and our future bride Megan Whelan for all your support. Come back soon Debbie who is on maternity leave. Congratulations to our newlyweds Rosie and Dan Shorten and welcome to our new boy in the kitchen—Colin Chih.

It was lovely to get the A Team together again to work on this book—I am indebted to Jacqui Small for the opportunity to indulge in more cakes; Rizzoli in New York for their enthusiasm; the ever so talented design team of Maggie Town and Beverly Price, for their art direction and design, and putting in many long hours; Janine Hosegood for her stunning photography and patience—and lunch everyday! (thanks, too, to Ralph and Max!); to the very pregnant, newly married (congratulations on both counts!) Kate John, also Judith Hannam and Madeline Weston for editing *Party Cakes*.

I would also like to thank my parents—Celia and Ralph—your support is appreciated more than you can know.

Thank you to Katie Ackland Snow—for being such a super nanny to my wonderful boys and allowing me to juggle being a working mother.